HOW TO
START A
BUSINESS

IN **2** WEEKS

HOW TO
START A
BUSINESS
IN
2
WEEKS

TONY EADES

First published in 2023 by Dean Publishing
PO Box 119
Mt. Macedon, Victoria, 3441
Australia
deanpublishing.com

Cataloguing-in-Publication Data
National Library of Australia
Title: How To Start a Business in Two Weeks
Edition: 1st edn
ISBN: 978-1-925452-71-6
Category: Business/Entrepreneurship

Printed in Victoria, Australia

MIX
Paper | Supporting
responsible forestry
FSC® C001695

Dedication

I'd like to dedicate this book to the over two million entrepreneurs across Australia who were brave enough to start a business, and the two million more that are yet to begin.

To the mums, wives and husbands, the partners and children who have supported these self-employed pioneers and believed in their success.

To my wife, Maria, and my wonderful children, Tim and Sarah-Jane, who have always motivated me to share my message in the media, on stage, and now in print.

CONTENTS

"We're here to put a dent in the universe. Otherwise why else even be here?"

STEVE JOBS

ARE YOU UP FOR THE CHALLENGE?

If you are reading this, then you are either an innovative pioneer thinking of starting your own business or someone who just hangs out in bookshops in search of inspiration, direction, or motivation. Well, the exciting thing is that, as an innovative pioneer and would-be business owner, you probably have those three attributes already.

Starting a business is probably one of the riskiest challenges you will ever undertake. Let's face it – the odds are against you before you even start, with an uncertain global economy, statistics showing that roughly a quarter of new businesses fail within the first year, and a marketplace that is becoming more and more competitive.[1]

But before you put this book down and place it back on the shelf, you should know there are also many reasons why there has never been a better time than today to start your own business.

THE RIGHT PLACE AT THE RIGHT TIME

I started my first business in the middle of a recession – yes, the so-called "recession we had to have." One sure thing about creating a new venture in a time of economic downturn is that it is recession-proofed from the very beginning, as opposed to a venture started in a boom time when we are probably a little carefree with our spending.

In Australia today, small businesses count for around 97 percent of all businesses – that's over 2 million businesses. By comparison, there are fewer than 100,000 medium to large businesses.[2] Can you imagine what our economy or unemployment rate would look like without small businesses?

Most people start a business because they are good at their job and want to go it alone, they have a great business idea, or they have secured a good product to market. But make no mistake – simply having a great product or being good at your job is not enough to create and run a successful small business. Running a business requires you to multitask and to wear a number of hats, including receptionist, sales professional, bookkeeper, and marketing manager – and that's all on top of your normal job. As your business grows, you will be able to outsource or employ people to take over some of these roles, but, initially, you'll be 'it', with no-one else to assist, and you'll need a clear understanding of all the key areas involved in your business.

Discipline and time management are going to be critical over the next two weeks as, together, we create your new business venture.

CREATING A BUSINESS, NOT JUST A JOB

It is vital that the business you choose is right for you and is something you really enjoy. Many people choose a business that is relevant to their profession or experience. For example, a primary school teacher might open a day care centre, or a hairdresser might open a hair salon, and so on. It is good to create a business in a field that you know a lot about so there is less to learn and, above all, you really know your product.

However, if you are looking for change and want to start a business that's not in keeping with your current line of work or experience, then take a long, hard look at yourself. This is the time to discover what you are really made of, deep down. What skills do you have that you haven't used yet? You have to believe in your product or service 100 percent, or no-one else will, and you'll find it hard to attract customers. Whatever the business you decide to create, you need to know your market. Is there a demand for your product or service, or is the market already oversaturated with competitors delivering something similar to what you are offering? Take a look into your imaginary crystal ball and fast forward five or ten years – will the demand for your product or service increase or decrease over this time?

In the late 1880s, Kodak was founded and became a giant in the photography industry in the 1970s. But an ignorance to new technology and a failure to adapt to changing market needs initiated Kodak's downfall, and they filed for bankruptcy in 2012.

Even though the first prototype of a digital camera was created in 1975 by Steve Sasson, an engineer working for Kodak, the company believed the market was in the photo film, chemical, and paper business and that is where it would stay.

In the 1980s, Stokes Music Land, a leading Perth retailer, captured the electronic organ market with the promise: "We'll have you playing today." The electronic music craze took off; stores opened in shopping centres all over the country, and the retailer became the leader in this field. Unfortunately, as trends changed and computers started to take over the market, the business failed to diversify and was only seen by consumers as the place to go for electronic organs, even though it also sold pianos and other instruments. Eventually, the demand for electronic organs disappeared, and with it went this retailer.

> It is important not just to think of the opportunities for your business right now but to make sure that there is a definite future for your business in the years to come.

There are basically two types of businesses: business to consumer (B2C) and business to business (B2B). The first category includes service businesses, such as hairdressers, electricians, or accountants, as well as retail shops, restaurants, and travel agents. The second type involves selling a product or service to another business, as is done by an advertising agency, a printer, or an IT company.

Whatever type of business you choose, the important thing to remember is that we are all basically in the same business. That's right – whether you are a butcher, a plumber, or a candlestick maker, we are all in the same business: the problem-solving business. Whatever product you make or whatever service you provide, it's all about people and fulfilling their needs. Take a jeweller for example – is he or she just selling rings and watches or, rather, fulfilling a need for a newly engaged couple to enable them to get married, or providing a reliable timepiece for a businessman to keep on schedule with his appointments? Start thinking of your business as a headache tablet. It is the cure for your customers' headaches or problems. There will be more about this later when we look at marketing your business.

THE MONEY-MAKING BUSINESS

When you are looking at starting a business, you should be motivated by three aims:

- Improving your lifestyle
- Achieving a better income
- Building goodwill and long-term value.

The first of these aims is pretty straightforward, and with it should come flexible working hours, being your own boss, and, as you become successful, the choice to decide which customers you want and which you don't.

The other two aims are about money, and, basically, they sum up the financial rewards you should receive for taking risks and putting in the extra effort needed to be self-employed instead of working for someone else. If you run your business well and focus on healthy margins – the difference between money coming in and money going out – you'll enjoy a healthy income.

So, what is goodwill? You may have heard it said that, when buying or creating a business, you need to have an exit strategy. Now, this is not an evacuation plan in case of a fire; it's a clear idea of what you intend to do when you have built your business as big as you want. You may have a succession plan to pass your business on to the next generation. Many of today's largest corporations were started this way. For most people, though, an exit strategy relates to when it comes time to sell the business – and this is where goodwill comes in.

When you start a business, the goodwill value is zero, and your goal is to build up this value as your business grows. Customers you attract, products you create, processes and systems you establish, your business name, logo, and brand, your sales growth and profitability – all of this and more add value to your goodwill.

The return you build in goodwill will depend on how much of 'you' is in the business. If the business needs you, and only you, to run it, then it makes selling the business to someone else down the line a little harder, unless you plan to stay on. With this in mind, calling your business Don's Landscaping or Bill's Butchers can also have an impact on the sale of your business, unless, of course, by chance, the buyer's name is also Don or Bill. There will be more about business names later.

To have the best chance of achieving valuable goodwill for your business, create that goodwill from day one, with systems and processes in place to ensure that the business can operate without you if need be. This, after all, is the same principle on which franchises, such as McDonald's, are built, where systems and processes, not just people, run the business. It's also a great foundation for saleability in the future, as your business develops and grows and you start hiring employees.

The final word on money is all to do with price. If you build your business on price alone, you really have nowhere to go. Being the cheapest doesn't build long-term client loyalty, and it can have a detrimental effect on your profit margin. Don't 'prostitute' your business by selling your products or services too low. Do your market research and find out what others are charging and what people are paying.

THE TWO-WEEK TIMEFRAME TO CREATE YOUR BUSINESS STARTS NOW

Once you have decided what type of business you want to create, and you have done a little research to make sure there is a market now and in the future for your products or services, *and* you have determined a future exit plan, it's time to begin!

Each chapter of this book equates to one day, so there are fourteen chapters in all, aimed at assisting you to create your business in just two weeks. The good news is that the days represented by Chapters 7 and 14 are kind of 'rest' days that we will use for reflection and, if you need it, a little catch-up time. If you start your business building on a Monday, these 'days off' will fall on a Sunday – your day of reflection and rest.

Try to read each chapter either the night before or first thing in the morning so you have most of the day to put everything you need to get done into action. Be sure to complete everything in each chapter before moving on to the next. Don't worry if it takes you longer than a day to complete a chapter. Completing all the tasks and building a strong foundation for your business to grow is the main goal.

So, if you're ready to go, let's begin a new chapter in your life with the excitement, challenges, and rewards of self-employment.

At the end of each chapter, you'll have a workbook to complete before moving on to the next chapter. Let's begin with 'why' (thanks Simon Sinek) you started this business in the first place. Think of it as your 'mission statement' that sums up the passion and motivation you have for wanting to start your own business.

YOUR MISSION
(SHOULD YOU CHOOSE TO ACCEPT IT)

What business are you creating?

ARE YOU UP FOR THE CHALLENGE?

Why now?

Why does it matter?

To whom does it matter?

....
....
....
....
....
....
....
....
....
....
....
....
....
....
....
....

Why am I the best person to start this business?

How will it make a difference?

What will this business look like five years from now?

"If you sell what you do, you're a vendor. If you sell why you do it, you're a brand."

SIMON SINEK

WHAT AM
I GOING
TO SELL?

The key to creating a successful, long-term business is all about creating a win-win situation. If you can provide a service or deliver a product to a customer so everyone benefits, then you really will have no need to actually 'sell' anything. It will simply sell itself.

Today's marketplace is full of businesses that promise the world but deliver very little. How many times have you seen an advertisement or read an article about a great product or service you could really use only to find that it didn't meet your expectations? The secret to success is to under promise and over deliver.

In Michael E. Gerber's bestselling book, *The E-Myth: Why Most Businesses Don't Work and What to Do About It*, we read about a hotel that stood out from its competitors by anticipating the guests' every need, from slippers by the fire to a hometown newspaper delivered every morning.[1] On Day 6 (Chapter 6 of this book), we will look at what is unique about your business: the thing that sets you apart from your competitors in the eyes of your customers. One clear advantage that you could easily have over your competitors could be customer service. It's the one thing that many businesses today overlook and the single factor that often determines whether a customer will come back again or even refer you to others.

At the end of this chapter, I'm going to ask you to write a list of exactly what you are going to provide for your customers. As you do this, you need to think in terms of 'features and benefits'. A 'feature' is the product or service, and a 'benefit' is what that feature actually does for the customer. For example, if you are going to provide a plumbing service, one of the benefits could be that you will offer a free water-saving home assessment with every call-out.

HOW MUCH DO I CHARGE?

Once you have your initial list of products or services, you need to work out how much you are going to charge your customers. If you charge too little, people may think that what you offer is of poor or inferior quality. If you charge too much, people may feel it is too expensive and will go elsewhere.

If you are selling a service, one of the best ways to determine your hourly rate is, firstly, to work out what you are worth. To do this, determine how much you would like to make as an annual salary. Suppose you have come from a job that paid you a salary of $50,000 per year, and you may want to make $100,000 as a business owner. Take the $100,000 and double it to cover tax, overheads, and so on. Then divide it by 48 (that's 52 weeks for the year, less four weeks for annual leave), and then again by 40 (the average number of working hours in a week). You should end up with a little over $104, so you could charge, say, $110 per hour for your services, plus GST.

If you are selling a product, the principle is slightly different. First, determine your cost price, which is the actual amount you need to pay for the product or, if you are manufacturing the product yourself, how much in raw costs it takes for you to create it. Next, you need to find out the price for which you can sell or retail the product, based on the current market. If a similar product is already available, find out the price at which it sells, and that will give you a guide. For this example, let's say that you can sell your product, the 'automatic prawn peeler', for $35, and it costs you an average of $15 to import or manufacture the product. Based on the previous example of receiving an annual salary of $100,000 doubled to cover overheads, tax, and so on, you would need to sell 10,000 peelers per year or 833 per month to achieve this.

There are a number of options to choose from when it comes to pricing, and you may end up selecting more than one, depending on the type of product or service you are providing.

Pricing strategies you may want to consider are described in the following paragraphs.

Price skimming – This is when a high price is charged for your new product or service, and people are willing to pay the extra for it. This pricing model appeals to the trendsetters of our world, who are always looking for the next big thing and are willing to pay the price to get it.

Penetration pricing – The opposite of price skimming is to introduce your product or service at a very low price so you can quickly gain a large share of the market. This may work well at the start; however, you will eventually have to put your prices up to sustain business, and, without brand loyalty, your customers may go elsewhere.

Buying a market position – This refers to the strategy where you buy your way into the market by offering free samples, introductory discounts, free services, or heavy discount coupons to attract new customers – for example, 50 cents off on a 69-cent purchase. This is a great model because it reduces any risk to the customer when it comes to using your product or service for the very first time.

Loss leader – In this case, you promote a few product items or a small service at a sizeable reduction to attract customers. Hopefully, by generating increased traffic and exposure, there will also be greater sales of your regular-priced lines as a result.

Multiple unit pricing – You might increase the size of your individual sales by offering an attractive discount and incentive for customers to consider a larger purchase. Online bookstore Amazon does this well by offering a second or third book – that complements the original purchase – along with savings on delivery by bundling the purchases together.

Suggested retail pricing – This strategy involves selling at prices that have been set by your suppliers. It can be a convenient option, especially in retail, because many product lines will be available pre-packaged and pre-priced.

Discount pricing – Think of your local discount store, where lower prices are offered as a trade-off for bland interiors, low customer service or sales assistance, and the efficiency of central checkouts. This model can also be applied to a service-based industry in which you would provide simpler, uncluttered solutions without the whistles and bells of your competitors.

Full-cost pricing – One of the most common and somewhat simple methods for setting a pricing structure is to work out the cost of producing your product or delivering your service and then add a flat fee or percentage to that cost as the margin of profit.

Keystone pricing – This method refers to the practice of setting the retail price at double the cost figure or, in other words, adding a 100 percent mark-up.

Price lining – This technique is used by most retail stores in which similar stock merchandise is sold over several different price ranges. For example, a hardware store may offer hammers in good, better, and best categories, with three different price points to match.

Competitive advantage – In this case, you set your prices in accordance with your competition. You can choose to set your prices equal to, above, or below those of your competitors, or you can promote a 'we-won't-be-undersold' strategy, through which you offer to meet or beat the prices of all your competitors.

Preseason pricing – There are many manufacturers that offer pricing discounts as incentives to buy early. Off-season specials may be a great way to profit in business on a year-round basis.

Price is no object – Finally, there are certain marketing situations in which the quality of or the need for a product or service far exceeds concerns regarding the price. For example, if a person needs a heart pacemaker, then he or she is probably not going to shop around or haggle over the price. In the same way, heavily discounted pricing is not what attracts customers to high-end jewellery or quality antiques.

THE POWER OF LEVERAGE

When it comes to running a business, one of the most powerful words you should come to learn and embrace is 'leverage'. In raw terms, this one word can make all the difference between having a small business operation that just ticks over and building a large, profitable operation that provides you with a comfortable, passive income.

There are only so many hours in the week, whichever way you look at it, and, of these, you can only physically work maybe 40 to 60 hours. Without any leverage in your business, the maximum output you can achieve is the direct output you can deliver, be it organising products, generating sales, or performing a service. This is fine when you are starting out. But how will your business grow, and what happens if you get sick or want to take a holiday?

Leverage is like adding cogs into your operation so, while the main wheel is turning hard, the outer wheels are spinning fast and free.

Adding leverage to your business and the products you sell is easier than you may think and can be achieved in a number of ways. For example, a website that sells your products 24 hours a day through an e-store is leverage and can provide you with passive income – that's money you receive without really doing anything. Contractors and employees add leverage to your business by performing the work for you, so too does cross selling other people's products or services for a commission and packaging what you do or sell so customers end up purchasing more than they actually need.

In short, leverage is just about getting more return for the work you put in. It is like getting two or three hours of income for every hour worked or increasing the value of your average customer purchase by 50 percent by adding value.

Once again, Amazon does this well by offering recommendations through nearly every part of their purchasing process. In fact, back in 2012, it was estimated by Forrestor analyst, Sucharita Mulpuru, that their conversion to sales from online recommendations could be as high as 60 percent.[2] Imagine the stats now?! Their algorithms are certainly some of the best in the world.

LET'S TALK ABOUT YOUR SUPPLY CHAIN

Whether you are selling a product or providing a service, you will probably need to have reliable suppliers to support your business. When it comes to the customer, the buck stops with you, so it is vital that you establish a solid supply chain early on and can maintain quality and keep up with demand.

Building strong relationships with your suppliers is as important as building strong relationships with your customers. As your business grows, there will be times when you really need to lean on your suppliers to deliver faster than normal turnarounds. Or you may even need them to reduce their prices so you can win a job. Your suppliers are your lifeline, and they are often a small business like yours, so treat them well, pay them on time, and thank them for the work they do for you.

It is always advisable to establish some form of agreement with your suppliers and have it well documented. The supply agreement should include expectations of quality, refund processes, trading terms, price increases, volume discounts, order turnaround, delivery, and so on. Make the agreement as short and as easy to read as possible so you don't need to spend too long on the legal stuff. If it gets too longwinded, you'll need a lawyer to write it, and your suppliers will need one just to read it.

Establish a network of suppliers rather than relying on just one. We did this early on in our online printing business, and it came in very handy when, at one stage, our main supplier became overwhelmed with work and pushed their delivery times from 5 to over 14 days. Our business model had been built on low cost and fast turnaround for our customers, so this wasn't acceptable. Luckily, we had two other suppliers that could deliver within the usual time frame, so we were able to direct our orders their way until our main supplier had their work demands under control. You also continually receive the best price when all suppliers are actively competing for your business.

Take a moment now to turn to the Business Workout section at the end of this chapter, find the page headed 'My Product/Service Offerings' and add your supplier or supplies to your list of core products or services that you will need to run your business. To find suppliers in your area, try an online search, or call your local Chamber of Commerce, because one of their members may well be the type of supplier you are looking for.

INTRODUCING THE 'PRODUCT MIX'

Establishing a good product mix is vital for creating brand harmony. You really cannot afford to be everything to everyone, so you need to look at your range of products and services and then trim down to just three or four that you know you can do really well. Your business and its brand need to be known primarily for its core products or services. For example, most people wouldn't go to McDonald's expecting a fine dining experience. The company has chosen a lane and sticks to it.

Let's say you are starting up a landscaping business called Create an Oasis. Your product mix could be landscaping design, landscaping projects, corporate consulting, and even a garden help desk. These products and services complement each other, thereby enhancing the brand promise and creating a 'cross sell' between them. For example, a customer may call on Create an Oasis to design a new garden for them, then may ask Create an Oasis to complete the project, and may finally call the Create an Oasis garden help desk on a future occasion for advice on adding new plants, maintaining the vibrant green lawn, or eradicating unwanted bugs and pests.

A good product mix helps your business focus only on what it is good at, instead of trying to be a jack-of-all-trades, and it adds to your recession proofing for the future. By having a split income source – that is to say, income coming in from different areas of your business – you are helping to protect your business for the future. When one area is not performing well, maybe due to an economic downturn or increased competition, the other areas of your business should still be delivering results. This is basically the 'pillar and bridge' principle: build a bridge with only two pillars and when one is lost or crumbles a little, the bridge falls down, but build the bridge with four or five pillars, and you can afford to lose one, even two or three, before the bridge is affected.

Before we begin Day 3, let's spend some time completing this Business Workout section. You will notice that there are three columns on the following page: one headed 'product or service', one headed 'customer benefit' and one headed 'supplier or supplies'. Think of what product or products, service or services your new business will provide and, next to each one, insert at least three benefits this will provide to the customer.

MY PRODUCT/SERVICE OFFERINGS

Product or Service	Customer Benefit*	Supplier or Supplies

* Remember, a 'benefit' is the value a customer receives from a product or service, as opposed to a 'feature', which is an objective detail about a product or service.

WHO AM I GOING TO SELL TO?

So, you've now got something to sell, but to whom are you going to sell it and where will you find them?

Most new business owners are convinced that their product or service is something everyone will want. I am yet to find a product that appeals to everyone, although global brands such as Google, Twitter, and Apple come close. Even market leaders, such as Coca-Cola, don't market their products to anyone and everyone – there is a defined audience that they want to reach and to whom they want to direct their message. In marketing, we call this their 'primary' or 'buyer persona'. For Coca-Cola, this core demographic is 13- to 17-year-olds, although, as we all know, these are not the only people who drink Coke. This more defined market allows Coca-Cola to design its television commercials, print ads, and point of sale posters to target and attract this market specifically. By default, it also captures a greater market, including the younger people who strive to be older and the older market who yearn to be younger. The company's philosophy is that Coke is not just a drink; it is a life experience, and that's why you will see Coke's television campaigns depicting first love and fun times, all of which are common experiences of a typical 13- to 17-year-old.

IDENTIFYING YOUR IDEAL CUSTOMER

In business terms, it is often said that your ideal customer is simply the person who is more likely to buy from you. Out of a population of approximately 26 million people in Australia, ranging in age from 1 to 100, including both male and female, gay and heterosexual, rich and poor, and so on, what segment of the population would be more attracted to your products or services than the rest?

For example, if we go back to our landscaping business, Create an Oasis, its core demographic might be 35- to 50-year-old, married, affluent women because this market takes pride in appearances and social status but is time poor. These people value a smart, stylish garden to enjoy and entertain in but don't have the time to maintain it. Once you can identify an 'ideal customer', it makes it easier to market to them because you can find out what they read, what they watch on television, or the radio station to which they listen.

The first step to finding out who might be your ideal customer is to look at your competitors. Do some market research of your own – go into your competitors' shops and see who's buying from them, take a look at their advertising and see who it's targeting, and ask your family, colleagues, and friends about why they would or would not buy from them. This valuable insight will not only help you determine who your own core demographic should be, but it will also assist you in defining how your business will differ from that of your competitors.

EXPANDING YOUR BOUNDARIES

If you had started your business 10 or 20 years ago, the majority of your customers would probably have come from within a 5 kilometre radius of your business. Nowadays, thanks to the internet and mobile phone technology, your customers could be anywhere.

Although this may sound like a bigger pool to tap into, it is also a far more competitive marketplace. In days gone by, your main competitors were probably two or three other businesses within your catchment area. Today, however, your competitors could include a mobile business based in the city but servicing all suburbs, an eBay seller with similar products to yours, or an online business based in India, direct selling a cheaper version of your products.

So, when it comes to identifying the customers you will be going after with your new business, you need to think traditional, territorial, and transglobal. Of course, not all products or services can be sold across the state, the country, or overseas. Take our Create an Oasis landscaping business for example – where do you think its boundaries would be set?

In effect, Create an Oasis could target customers traditionally in its local area for landscape design and construction, customers territorially for its corporate consulting services, and then even transglobally for its online garden help desk. The power of the internet is such that it is not merely a parking ground for your business website; it is a communication platform for sharing information, selling products, creating forums, streaming video tutorials, publishing informative podcasts, and even talking to potential customers via email, wherever they might live.

LAYING YOUR FOUNDATIONS FOR BUSINESS BUILDING

The foundation or backbone of every business is its customer base. It doesn't matter how good your products are, how smart your shop looks, or how efficient your service is, without customers, your business won't amount to a hill of beans. So, it goes without saying that protecting this core asset should be paramount from day one.

In business today, you need to own your customers because if you don't, someone else will. By 'own' them, I mean build a relationship so strong that they won't want to go anywhere else and will remain loyal to your business.

To help you do this, you will need to establish a system for creating and maintaining your customer list. This is called a database. The good news is that when it comes to building a database, modern technology becomes your best friend with off-the-shelf, easy-to-use products that virtually do it for you.

Here are six database solutions that you could use for your new business (note that the list is up-to-date and relevant at the time of writing):

- Microsoft Dynamics
- Salesforce
- HubSpot CRM
- Insightly
- Zoho

A good database system, set up from day one and maintained regularly, is vital to the ongoing operation and future success of your business.

Spend a few minutes now examining the database systems listed above or other popular database programs and decide which one appeals to you the most. You can then download a trial version and get started. If it's not what you had in mind, then save or export your data and try another one.

WANT TO BUY SOME CUSTOMERS?

Now, don't think we are talking about bribery and corruption, although a lot of advertising methods used by some 'direct sell' businesses could easily fall into that category. To get your customer database started, it is possible for you to buy an existing database of customers who fit your products or services.*

We have already determined who your 'ideal customer' is, so, using this important information, you can go to a company like Impact Lists or Dun & Bradstreet and request to purchase a database of all people that fit these criteria within a set catchment area – say, 5 to 10 kilometres from your point of business.

The database provider will then supply you with a quote, including an overall count of how many people fit the criteria requested, how many of them have actual contact names, and options for purchasing just the mailing information, the telemarketing details, or both. These companies have already done the hard work for you, combining data from the current census and other sources, then verifying it, and, finally, putting it all into a handy, easy to import spreadsheet. For around a dollar per entry, you can 'buy' these customers and import them straight into your new database program. It is

---

* It is important to ensure that any database you purchase is created from an 'opt in' source, which means that those contacts have opted in to receive information from you.

important to ensure that any database you purchase is created from an 'opt in' source, which means that those contacts listed have opted in to receive new information, otherwise you could be in trouble for 'spamming' when you send your first promotion.

Your database will then be ready to use as your own in-house marketing tool, enabling you to send out personalised information about your business to the right people, to call them on the phone, and then to turn them into actual paying customers – but more about that later.

YOU'RE ONLY AS GOOD AS YOUR NETWORK

To help create a strong customer base to get your business started, you need to do a little networking. Networking has become the buzzword when doing business in the modern world. Your success is directly proportional to how 'connected' you are.

We could spend a whole chapter, or even the entire book, on the subject of networking because it's really that powerful.

So, what is networking? *Macquarie Dictionary* describes networking as, "The establishing of communication links with other people as a means of exchanging ideas and information." Business contacts and knowledge gained from experience are among the types of information that can be exchanged.

Networking is also a tremendous way to build some leverage into your business from the beginning. Let's face it – from day one, the business is probably only going to consist of you, and there is only so much one person can do. Remember, you are already wearing the general manager's hat and the salesperson's hat, as well as being the person providing all of the products and services of the business, so any leverage will really come in handy.

Your network is really a group of businesspeople who are in noncompeting professions, with some products or services that can be complementary to each other's businesses. In plain terms, let's look again at our landscaping business, Create an Oasis. If these landscapers were to actively start networking, they could make contact with, say, a real estate business, a furniture retailer, and a nursery. Forming an alliance with these businesses would help create new business for the landscapers, including customers whose homes may have just listed with the realtor and who may be needing to add some appeal and value to their property. The furniture retailer and the plant nursery could promote Create an Oasis to its customers as a complementary service to their existing products.

So, how do you get started? Well, there are a few easy ways you can kickstart your networking.

CHAMBER OF COMMERCE

There will be a Chamber of Commerce in your local area that hosts and organises a calendar of networking events, business functions, and training workshops. Membership is usually around $500 per year, and, for that, you will receive a weekly events newsletter, inclusion within the online local business directory, and invitations to events as they happen.

In my experience, I have found the Chamber of Commerce to be more of a way to connect with businesses and cross sell each other's services than a direct source for customer leads and actual work.

BUSINESS NETWORKING GROUPS

Independent local Business Network International (BNI) groups or chapters are being established all over the country, and each follows a specific format, much like a franchise system. Members are encouraged to promote other members' products and services and, in so doing, source leads for other businesses in the group.

Although the meetings are well structured, you may feel overwhelmed with your obligations to your chapter, including attending all weekly meetings (you are only allowed to miss three before potentially being expelled from the group), lead generation for other members, and an initial membership fee of close to $1000.

LinkedIn

The first of the popular online networking platforms we will discuss is LinkedIn. With LinkedIn, you create a free account, establish a business profile, and then seek out people you know or would like to know, who are also members. By introducing yourself and receiving an acceptance, you become 'linked' not only to that person but also to his or her network. It doesn't take long for you to establish a network of hundreds of connections for sharing ideas, joining discussion forums, and generating leads.

Meetup and Eventbrite

Founded in 2002, Meetup is a social media platform for hosting and organising events. You can search by interest, topic, or type and then add your location.

Similarly, Eventbrite allows you to find the best business events in your area and online. Networking is a great way to connect with other like-minded people and grow your business.

START NETWORKING!

You can, of course, just write a list of all the businesses in your local area that you think may have complementary products or services and make an appointment to meet for a coffee and a chat.

Take a moment now to try out the networking platforms we've discussed. Don't worry too much at this stage about building your profile because that will be covered later.

Let's now complete the Business Workout section for 'Who Am I Selling to?'. You'll notice that there are five blank sections headed 'My Competitors', and your task today is to complete these sections by researching your customers online (by doing an online search for your product or service), in your local newspaper, on LinkedIn, and in person by visiting competitors in your area directly.

There is also one added section to complete today, your 'Competitor Matrix'. Plot your competitors first on this matrix against the quality and cost axis. Then plot where you think your new business will sit in comparison to these competitors.

MY COMPETITORS

Business name	What do you like?*	Website URL

* What would stand out to you about this business if you were a potential customer?

THE COMPETITOR MATRIX

	HIGH	PRICE	
LOW			HIGH
QUALITY			QUALITY
	LOW	PRICE	

Add a dot with the name of the competing business next to it and then plot where you think the market perception is for that business, that is, is the business considered high quality with a high price? If so, add them to the top right quadrant.

IT'S ALL IN A NAME

It's day four already in our two-week business startup, and it's time to get a little creative. Just like what happens when you bring home a newborn baby or pet puppy, it's time to give your new business a name of its own. So, let's spend today looking at why your business name is important and how to go about creating one.

LET'S NAME HIM AFTER MUM AND DAD

Like many startup businesses, you may consider mixing your name with your partner's name, and you may come up with something like Jotom (joining together Joe and Tom) or Bevmax (Beverley and Max). Although this may mean something to you – and your partner – it says very little to your customers. Your business name should communicate what you do or how you do it rather than who's running the business.

The name should be as short as possible. Long business names just do not perform as well as shorter names because they are harder for potential customers to remember or even spell when searching on the internet. Imagine Qantas today if it was still marketed under its full name of Queensland and Northern Territory Aerial Services.

Try to avoid generic names like Go-Green Printers or Cars Online because these will be harder to register as a business and domain name. The particulars of what you do can be described in your positioning statement or Unique Selling Proposition (USP), so they don't need to be in your actual name – more about this on Day 6.

Ideally, you want a one-word or two-word name that will enable you to eventually define the product or service you offer to your demographic. For example, think of what Kleenex is to tissues, Hoover is to vacuum cleaners, and Google is to internet search engines. These are one-word company names that have been positioned so well that they now own their product categories. We don't say, "Pass the tissues;" we say, "Pass the Kleenex." And we don't say, "I'll search for that on the internet;" we say, "We'll Google it."

Today, the more creative the name, the better chance you will have of registering it and securing an appropriate domain name. Imagine if the owners of our landscaping business, Create an Oasis, had wanted to name the business Landscaping Australia or Great Gardens. They probably would have had a problem registering the business name or the web domain.

Although Create an Oasis doesn't say anything about landscaping, the company's USP, "Great gardens in half the time," says it all.

WHAT DO OTHERS THINK OF OUR NEW NAME?

Now it's time to get creative and start brainstorming some potential business names. Start with a list of ten or twenty ideas and show these to your friends, family, and business associates for them to comment and select their favourites. By doing this, you get some instant market research from a mixed-age audience that is hopefully also representative of your future customer base.

For every name you add to your list, you need to ask yourself whether it creates a positive feeling for your business, is memorable, can't be confused with a competitor's business name, and is available to register.

You can instantly check the availability of any business name through the Australian Securities and Investments Commission's (ASIC's) free company name search at www.asic.gov.au. You can also check whether the domain name is available. Your domain name is practically your online street address, so registering a domain name as well as a business name is important. Today, every business should have a web presence.

Let's pause here and brainstorm some potential business names...

IT'S ALL IN A NAME

Complete the table below with 10 potential business names, limiting them to one or two words.

	Business Name	URL	/10
1.			
2.			
3.			
4.			
5.			
6.			
7.			
8.			
9.			
10.			

Next, check the names for their availability as a domain name using https://www.godaddy.com. For example, if you had a business name like Cool Bananas, then search 'Cool Bananas' in the search window and see what is available. Tick the column marked URL if there is a suitable domain name available, or a cross if not.

Once you have the completed list, go online to ASIC and see if each name is available for registration. Highlight each one that you can register as a business name - remember, the business name doesn't have to exactly match the 'trading' name. For example, if your brand name is 'Cool Bananas', you could register the business name with ASIC as 'Cool Bananas Australia' or 'Cool Bananas Group'.

Now send the list of potential business names to your friends and close associates for them to give you some independent feedback. Ask them to rate the names from one to ten, one being their first preference. Add all of the feedback numbers together for each name, and the lower the final number, the better the choice. It also is important to ask them to make a short comment about why they selected the names they did because this will help you determine your final selection.

NAME IT AND FRAME IT

At this stage, you should have about three or four potential names for your new business venture. To trim the list further, you should now conduct a 'trademark search'. A trademark protects your name and logo against others copying your business concept and setting themselves up in direct competition to you. If your business is a fashion brand or consumer product, then it is vital that you check its availability, not only in Australia but internationally as well.

For Australian trademark searches, go online to www.ipaustralia.gov.au and use the free trademark database search. Before you conduct your search, you need to determine the category or class into which your product or service fits. For example, if you have a clothing label, then you will be searching for availability under class 25: "clothing, footwear, headgear." This is important, as your preferred business name may already be trademarked but under a different classification than the one you want.

Simply cross out the names that are not eligible for a trademark. Now, with the remaining names, it is down to you to make a final decision on which will become the new identity of your business. The name will be with you for many years to come, so, although it may sound good now, will it be as fresh in five or ten years' time? A business may freshen or modernise its logo or brand every five to ten years, but, generally, you should avoid changing the name because it will form the heart of your goodwill.

Congratulations! You should now have a name for your business that is strong, says what your business does, and is not like any others in your market space. Now it's time for a little paperwork.

"If you fail to plan, you are planning to fail!"

BENJAMIN FRANKLIN

THE BORING STUFF

If you are an accountant, financial advisor, or just love to exist in a world of Excel spreadsheets, you'll probably find this chapter the most exciting. As for the rest of us, it's time to dot the i's and cross the t's to make sure the business structure is watertight and strong enough to withstand growth into the future.

Let's begin today by looking at the various business structure options available to you and the benefits that each provides.

EVERY MASTERPIECE NEEDS A STRONG FRAME

Think of yourself as a 19th century painter who is just about to begin his next masterpiece. You have an idea of what you intend to create, so you need to make sure the frame that will display it is big enough and strong enough to support it.

In business terms, the 'frame' is really the business structure, and, in today's market, there are six options from which to choose:

- Sole trader
- Partnership
- Company
- Unit trust
- Discretionary trust
- Superannuation fund entity

Let's look at the pros and cons of each structure in more detail.

SOLE TRADER

The sole trader model is probably the easiest and least expensive way to set up a business. In simple terms, you are an individual trading as the business, for example, Sam Smith trading as Spotless Car Cleaners. The downside is that you are not protected, and, therefore, you are directly exposed to risk if anything bad should happen to your business. There are also limited means for reducing your income tax because, basically, what the business earns is what you earn.

PARTNERSHIP

A partnership is generally set up when two or more people are involved in the business operations. This could be two individuals or a husband and wife who decide to go into business together. Unlike a sole trader, the partnership model can have its own name rather than incorporating the names of the partners, for example, Spotless Investments trading as Spotless Car Cleaners. Partnerships allow for your income to be split between both partners, which can provide tax advantages over a single sole trader structure.

On the downside, the costs of setting up a partnership are greater than the costs for a sole trader because a partnership agreement is usually drawn up by a lawyer to protect both partners. Things can also become difficult if one partner decides they want to move away from the business or if there is a stalemate on a particular decision. In a fifty-fifty partnership, both partners need to agree for any decision to be taken and for the business to move forward; otherwise, an independent, third-party adjudicator is appointed to make the decision.

COMPANY

A company is probably the most preferred and safest structure for businesses, although there are associated set-up costs involved in this model. When you form a company, you decide on a company name, which could be, for example, Spotless Group Pty Ltd, trading as Spotless Car Cleaners. Instead of the owners being the legal entity, as in the sole trader and partnership models, the company is the legal entity, and the owners become shareholders. This option is the ideal solution if you have three or more people involved in the business operations; however, it can work just as well with just one owner. From an income perspective, the owners or shareholders receive 'dividends' and 'drawings' as well as wages.

The standard company tax rate is 25 percent, so all income received by the business is already franked at this rate. If you are in a higher tax bracket and personally pay, say, 45 percent tax, your tax rate on any income from dividends can be reduced by the 25 percent already paid by the company, so you could pay just 20 percent tax on these earnings instead of the original 45 percent.

As a company, you are also bound by certain regulations, like having a regular board meeting, and your ability to trade depends on whether the company is solvent.

UNIT TRUST

This model is often used when you are entering a joint venture operation with another business or for buying investments when more than one person is involved. With a unit trust, the entity buys the shares in a business operation or investment – let's say that this is equivalent to 100 units. Each beneficiary of the trust is then awarded blocks of units, either in equal shares or in accordance with their commitment to the operation. Units can then be easily sold or traded down the track without affecting the operations of the business.

A unit trust, like a company, is a legal entity, so the owners or beneficiaries are quite protected from risks associated with the actual business operations, provided there is a corporate trustee in place.

DISCRETIONARY TRUST

Similar to a unit trust, a discretionary trust brings together individuals who, together, control the assets of a business. However, with this model, the individuals are usually family members. The set-up would be something like this: Smith Family Trust trading as Spotless Car Cleaners. The operations of the trust are decided upon by a trustee, which could be one of the family members or could even be a company acting as the trustee.

There are good income tax advantages to having a discretionary trust because the business profits can be distributed among all beneficiaries, including children. Those with little or no income can be allocated a portion of the income, helping keep individual tax rates to a minimum. On the downside, discretionary trusts can be a little expensive to set up from the start but as the business grows – and the profits with it – the financial benefits will generally outweigh the initial investment.

With all of the business structure options mentioned, it is strongly advised that you speak to your accountant or financial advisor to discuss which option is best for you.

This table shows the advantages of each structure.

SUMMARY TABLE FOR APPROPRIATE STRUCTURE

Source: Richards Financial Services

	Sole Investor	Partnership	Private Company	Unit Trust	Discretionary Trust	Superannuation Fund
Administered by	Individual	Partners	Directors	Trustee	Trustee	Trustee
Responsible to	n/a	Partners	Shareholders	Unit holders	Appointer	Members
Cost to establish and run	Low	Fairly low	Higher	Higher	Higher	Higher
Protection of assets from outside risks/claims	No	No	Only if owned by discretionary trust	Only if owned by discretionary trust	Yes	Yes
Maximum tax rate	Up to 45% plus Medicare levy	Up to 45% plus Medicare or 26% if Partner is a Company	26% if profit retained Small business	Up to 45% or if unit holder is company 26%	Up to 45% or 30% if able to distribute to a company beneficiary	15% if a complying fund (45% if non-complying)
Potential for slitting income	No	Between partners	Between shareholders	Between unit holders	Between beneficiaries	No, but reduces members tax
Streaming of income	No	Limited	No	Dependent on trust deed	Yes, subject to trust deed	No
Taxable capital gains	Paid by individual	Paid by partners	Paid by company	Paid by unit holder	Paid by beneficiaries	Paid by trustee
Access to CGT discount for assets held greater than 12 months	Yes – 50%	Yes – 50%	No	Yes: If unit holder individual 50% If unit holder is SMSF 33% If unit holder is company 0%	Yes: If benef. individual 50% If benef. is SMSF 33% If benef. is company 0%	Yes – 33%
Other realised capital profits	Not taxed	Not taxed	Taxed as an unfranked dividend to shareholder	May be taxed as capital gain	Not taxed	15% in a complying in a complying business
Can losses be distributed?	Yes	Yes	No	No	No	No
Tax-free 'tithing'	No	No	No	Via family trust unit holder	Yes, subject to trust deed	No
Interest-free loan relatives	Not taxed as income	Not taxed as income	May be taxed as deemed dividend	Not taxed as income	Not taxed as income	Not permitted
Flexibility	Poor	Fairly poor	Fair	Good	Very good	Fairly poor
Admission for new parties	New structure is required	Usually permitted	Usually permitted	Usually permitted	May be difficult for non-family members	Usually permitted
Changing ownership	n/a	Partnership interest	Shares	Units	By appointer	n/a

*Subject to legislative changes and meeting the Small Business Entity definition as defined by the ATO. Please discuss your particular circumstances with your accountant.

Please Note: Many of the comments in this publication are general in nature and anyone intending to apply the information to practical circumstances should seek professional advice to independently verify their interpretation and the information's applicability to their particular circumstances.
Liability limited by a Scheme approved under the Professional standards Act 1994 (NSW)

TIME TO GET YOUR DUCKS IN A ROW

In the previous chapter, you brainstormed, searched, and hopefully finalised a business name. Now it is time to register that name.

To do this, you need to either use the online Business Registration Service (https://register.business.gov.au/) or ask your accountant to register the business name for you. The cost at the time of writing is $98 for three years; however, prices will fluctuate over time. Using the online service, you can also apply for an Australian Business Number (ABN) if you haven't already. An ABN is a unique number that identifies your business and is used for keeping track of transactions for GST and other tax purposes. You'll also need a tax file number if you don't have one already.

If your preferred name is not available, rather than choosing something totally different, remember you can simply add 'Australia' or 'Group' to the original name. For example, if the preferred name of Spotless Cleaning is unavailable, you could instead use Spotless Cleaning (Australia), Spotless Cleaning Group, or even The Spotless Cleaning Group.

Be sure to have your chosen business structure in place before you apply for your business name because you will be asked for the name of the people or entity that will be operating this business.

Once you have registered your business name, you

will receive a certificate of registration and an **ABN** (if applicable).

Now it's time for the domain name: the online address that people will use to find you and your business. You can register your domain with a registrar of your choice. Different providers will offer different packages and pricing, so it can pay to shop around.

Ideally, you should register not only the Australian domain (.com.au) but also the international domain (.com), as well as any similar domains (such as .au, .net and .net.au). All of these domains can be set up to point to the one main business website.

When you register your domain name, you will be given a variety of hosting options. You will eventually need three: domain hosting, email hosting, and web hosting. It is important that you select a domain and email hosting package at this stage because your emails will run with your new domain. For example, if you have registered www.spotlesscleaners.com.au, then your email addresses could be sam@spotlesscleaners.com.au or info@spotlesscleaners.com.au.

Finally, you need a trademark, which will be registered with **IP** Australia. This part of the set-up can be completed with just your business name, thus, protecting it from any similar or opposing names in the future. Alternatively, you can wait until your logo and brand have been created and then register the name, logo, and identity all together in the one application.

This would then protect not only your name but also your brand, its colours, and even your Unique Selling Proposition (USP) if you include it as a part of your logo. There is more about creating your USP in the next chapter.

LOCATION! LOCATION! LOCATION!

Every time you buy a house, your local real estate agent tells you there are only three things you need to look at: location, location, and location. When it comes to business, it's much the same – where will you run your business from? If you are opening a shop, kindergarten, or business that needs walk-in customers, then your location has probably already been determined.

If, however, you are setting up a business that requires just an office from which to run the operations, then you have a few choices to make. Are you going to run the office from home, rent some office space, or sign up for a virtual office?

HOME OFFICE

Due to low ongoing costs and no long-term lease commitments, this is an attractive option for a startup business. If you like this solution, make sure you can allocate a dedicated room in your home to your business operations, and, ideally, it should be one that can be easily shut off from the rest of the house. This will give you privacy when you need it and also create a clear divide between 'work' and 'home'.

It is also strongly advised that you apply for a PO Box at your local post office so you do not need to publicly advertise your home address to customers. Instead, people simply send all correspondence to your PO Box, and you collect the mail daily, weekly, or whenever suits you.

VIRTUAL OFFICE

The virtual office concept, whereby you have a smart city address and phone number but have all of your calls redirected to your mobile or home office, is growing in popularity. As a virtual office client, you can utilise companion offices throughout Australia, or even the world, if the serviced office company you choose has multiple locations. At a small additional cost, the virtual office solution also gives you access to a day suite or boardroom for meetings and client presentations as required.

OFFICE SPACE

You can rent office space – furnished or unfurnished – directly yourself, or you can share existing office space, or you can take a serviced office. The first two options will require a commitment in the form of a lease for at least 6 to 12 months, whereas a serviced office can be leased for as little as a month at a time.

Regardless of where you decide to have your office, you should seriously consider having a 1300 phone number. A 1300 number allows you to have one number for the whole of Australia, and it goes with you if you decide to move offices down the track. It is also easier to remember than a generic landline number and gives you a more professional business image. The added benefit of a 1300 number is that you receive a detailed monthly report of your call activity, showing who called, when, and from where. Contact a company like Zintel, for example, to secure a 1300 phone number for your business.

PLANNING THE JOURNEY

A business without a business plan is like a ship without a rudder, relying on the natural elements of wind and current to steer it on its voyage. But, like a ship without a rudder, you also run the risk of the winds blowing the wrong way and running you aground.

A business plan is basically a map of where you see your business going and how you intend to get there. It is important to understand that just as your business will evolve and change, so should your business plan, with you reviewing it every year and making adjustments as needed to stay on course.

When the NASA Apollo missions left Cape Canaveral and the John F. Kennedy Space Center for the Moon, what percentage of the time do you think they were directly on course? You would, perhaps, hope that it would be 70 or 80 percent of the time, but, on average, it was just 13 percent. Instead of going in a straight line from the Earth to the Moon, the rocket tacked its way across space, affected by winds and atmospheric currents.

On day nine, we will roll up our sleeves and fully develop our business plan. In the meantime, however, we need to create a 'startup business plan'. Think of this as the architectural plan for constructing a building, whereas the full business plan will be the equivalent of the completed building with all its fixtures, fittings, and tenants.

Your startup business plan should include the elements discussed in the following paragraphs.

PURPOSE AND BACKGROUND

Generally, business plans begin with a statement of purpose that outlines what the business is about and what it will offer to the market. This section also includes background on how and why you came up with the idea for the business and the type of customers you will be targeting.

BUSINESS STRUCTURE AND MARKET ENVIRONMENT

The business structure shows who will be involved in the operations and what they will be doing. As in the case of the Apollo missions, you need to know who is commanding the rocket, who is copilot, and who is in the engine room, as well as who your ground crew are. In business, your ground crew could include your accountant, your business coach, and so on.

We also need to take a look at the market environment into which you are about to step. This will include any major competitors and market trends for your type of product or service.

You can also extend this to what is called a SWOT

analysis, where you look at strengths, weaknesses, opportunities, and threats that may affect the business.

OPERATIONAL PLAN

This is where you identify the real mechanics of the business – what will make it tick. First up would be your product or service mix – what are you going to be selling or providing so as to earn a profit? Then comes the marketing – how will you tell people about your products or services so that they can buy from you? Finally, the financial plan – how much will it cost to set up your business and operate it successfully?

BUILDING YOUR TEAM

As you grow your business and look to start hiring staff, it is critical to do this right. To understand all conditions relating to employing people, like wages and awards, leave entitlements, employment conditions, ending employment, and so on, go to Fair Work Ombudsman at www.fairwork.gov.au.

Let's complete the Business Workout section with a checklist of all the items we've discussed that now need to be actioned, as well as your startup business plan template.

THE BORING STUFF

Complete the following checklist before moving on to the next chapter.

Business Set-up Task	Tick
Business structure, for example, sole trader, partnership, and so on	
Register the business name	
Apply for your Australian Business Number (ABN) + tax file number (TFN)	
Domain name registered	
Domain and email hosting completed	
Trademark applied for (if applicable)	
Location: home, office, or virtual (with a PO Box)	
Office phone number, for example, 1300...	

THE 'STARTUP' BUSINESS PLAN

On Day 9, you will develop a full business plan; for now, we're going to create a 'startup business plan'.

Purpose and Background

Summarise 'Your Mission *(should you choose to accept it)'* from Day 1 into one paragraph.

....

....

....

....

....

....

....

....

....

....

....

....

....

Business Structure

Who's wearing what hats in this new business venture? If you don't have anyone specifically, then add your name in multiple roles – it's not uncommon for a startup entrepreneur to wear many hats.

Business Role	Name
Chief Executive Officer	
Chief Operating Officer	
Financial Controller	
Marketing Director	
Sales Director	

You should also think about your potential 'ground crew' who can help support you as you start your business. You can complete these roles as needed and as your business grows.

Business Role	Name
Accountant	
Business Coach	
Mentor	
Solicitor	
Personal Trainer	

Major Competitors

List here some competing businesses already playing in your space.

....

....

....

....

....

....

....

....

....

....

SWOT Analysis

A SWOT analysis looks at your current Strengths and Weaknesses – generally related to internal elements of your business. For example, a Strength might be that you have in-depth knowledge of your industry, while a Weakness may be that you lack technical expertise to, say, build a website.

Opportunities and Threats are external factors that may impact your business. For example, an Opportunity may be that you are introducing a new product that is lower cost than what is available right now, while a Threat may be that rising interest rates may impact the appetite for your potential customers to buy.

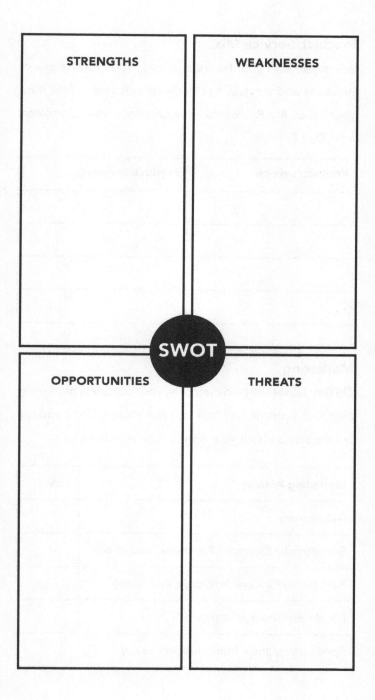

Product/Service Mix

When you start your business, it is good to have a mix of products and services to offer your customers. Add here your list of *'My Product/Service Offerings'* you completed from Day 2.

Product/Service	Product/Service

Marketing

On Day 12, we will be developing your complete marketing plan, but, for now, let's look at a few ideas on how you will tell the world about your new business venture.

Marketing Activity	Tick
Networking	
Social media (LinkedIn, Facebook, and so on)	
Paid media (Google AdWords, and so on)	
Local newspaper advertising	
Sponsorship (local footy club and so on)	

Financial Planning

Most startup businesses are bootstrapped; however, it is important to have an idea of how much investment you will need to get your business up and running.

Business Investment	Budget
Logo design (est. $500–$1000)	
Website (est. $500–$5000)	
Company vehicle (est. $20,000+)	
Equipment to run your business (specific tools, machinery, and so on)	
The boring stuff (est. $1000–$2000)	
Office costs (if not operating at home)	
Phone, internet, and computer	
Marketing budget	
Stock to sell	
Proposed Investment	$

"If your business is not on the internet, then your business will be out of business."

BILL GATES

DAY

6

WHAT'S REALLY UNIQUE ABOUT MY BUSINESS?

Let's say that you are in the market for a new car. You've done the research, and you know what make and model you're after: a Toyota Camry, for example.

You now search online for a Toyota dealer in your area, and you quickly find that there are ten to select from. So, what is it that makes you choose one over the other? It's a new car, so you know that the price will be about the same at each dealership, and they have all got the car you want on display in their showrooms. Then you see that at one of the dealerships, you get a guaranteed trade-in value for any licensed car when you buy from that particular dealer. This is welcome news because you need to sell your early model Corolla to make way for the new Camry.

You can make your own customers' buying decisions so much easier by offering something different from your competitors – something unique and meaningful. We call this your Unique Selling Proposition, or USP.

CREATING AND EXPLOITING YOUR USP

Invented back in the early 1940s by Rosser Reeves of the Ted Bates & Co. advertising agency, the USP was originally used as a means to try to persuade customers to switch brands.

In today's competitive marketplace, you must be 'unique' and 'fill a special niche' to be successful in business. Having a USP will enable your business to improve its positioning and will drive your success through focused, tactical marketing. Your USP should clearly set you apart from your competitors and should have your prospects saying, "Oh yes, I've heard of you. You're the company that…"

So, let's look at the following five elements for creating and exploiting your USP.

USE YOUR BIGGEST BENEFITS

Your prospects really don't care if you offer the best price, service, or quality, so you have to explain to them exactly 'why' that is important to them. People buy benefits and not features, so identify and list three big benefits that a customer would receive from owning your product or using your service.

BE UNIQUE

Your USP should separate you from your competitors, so it needs to be unique. It needs to create a 'buying criteria' so your business is clearly the logical choice for the customer in search of your product or service.

Your USP should create desire and urgency. It could be related to your product, your offer, or your guarantee – for example, "If you do not believe that our product is the best value on the market, we will refund your money."

SOLVE AN INDUSTRY 'PERFORMANCE GAP'

Many businesses today base their USP on a gap between the current situation and the desired objectives. This is commonly known as a 'performance gap'. So, find a hole in the industry, and fill it with your USP.

MAKE IT MEANINGFUL AND MEMORABLE

Create a one-liner – a statement that is powerful, memorable, and, above all, measurable. Federal Express has a USP that says, "When it absolutely, positively has to be there overnight." Now, that's powerful, easily remembered, and certainly measurable. Once you have your USP, you need to include it on all of your marketing materials, from your business cards to your advertising.

DELIVER ON THE PROMISE

Finally, it is vital that you can deliver your brand promise. Federal Express had to develop systems to make sure it delivered on its promise, and you need to do the same. A good, strong USP can deliver real success or, equally, failure if the business doesn't live up to its promise.

Domino's Pizza identified a performance gap in the marketplace when research found that people didn't want a hotter, tastier, or cheaper pizza – they ultimately wanted a pizza that would be delivered faster. Customers said that if they ordered a pizza, they didn't want to wait an hour or so for it to be delivered. Domino's identified with this and came up with the USP: delivered in "30 minutes or it's free." It was a simple statement that made them the leading choice for pizza in the US, literally, overnight.

THE POWER OF THE PROMISE

Your USP, like the Domino's example, can be a powerful positioning statement that reduces or even removes the customer risk of doing business with you. It also demands a commitment from you and your employees to deliver on the promise. In the case of Domino's, however, this became a problem. In 1989, it was claimed a Domino's driver, due to rushing to deliver a pizza within 30 minutes, had been involved in an accident that left a woman with severe injuries.[1] This, along with other similar accidents, forced Domino's to eventually remove and replace its USP.

So, what is unique about your business, your product, or your service?

First, we need to move away from price being the single reason people buy from you. If price is your only motivator, then you really have nowhere to go if a competitor enters the market with similar pricing or introduces a 'value add' that is more appealing to the customer. Being purely the cheapest doesn't build long-term customer loyalty and certainly doesn't add value to your brand.

Building a strong and meaningful brand over time acts as a barrier to entry for competitors who want to enter your market. If price is your only point of difference, it is easy for anyone to enter the market and steal your market share literally overnight by merely offering a cheaper alternative.

Look at your current competitors and find a niche that would set you apart from them and make buying from you the logical choice for any prospective customer. The following are a few ideas to consider.

RISK REVERSAL

When a potential customer is considering buying a product or service from a business that they haven't used before, the risk is generally on their side. There are no guarantees that the product or service will meet their expectations and if it doesn't, they are the ones that lose out. By offering a money-back, satisfaction guarantee, you are in effect reducing or even eliminating the customer's risk of trying your product or service for the first time. You are standing by everything you sell, and, basically, the buck stops with you. If a customer is unhappy with your product, they can return it for a full refund, no questions asked.

FASTER TO MARKET

In a world where we are all time-poor, any promises of a faster or more reliable delivery can provide a great USP. Search online for customer forums about your competitors or their products or services, for comments on problems in quality or delivery. From here, you can form your USP around a solution to these problems and, thus, build your business around the shortfalls of your competitors.

FIRST TO MARKET

Trendsetters thrive on having the first of anything, especially in the area of technology. Apple has built its own success around this philosophy and, eventually, achieved greater capitalisation than Microsoft. People will queue overnight and pay over the odds to be the first to own a newly released product or service. If you can secure an edge over your competitors and be the first to release a product or service to market, you will establish a definitive advantage.

MAKE DOING BUSINESS WITH YOU MORE EXCLUSIVE

A travelling businessman was visiting a colleague in a big city and organised to meet him for dinner. The colleague had arranged a booking at a local Italian restaurant and mentioned that this restaurant was so exclusive that bookings had to be made weeks in advance. After the meal, the businessman commented to his friend that, although the food was good and the atmosphere nice, the restaurant didn't seem so different that it would command such popularity. His colleague told him to wait until later in the evening, and he would see why the restaurant was so popular. Towards the end of the evening, a larger than life Italian woman emerged from the kitchen and promptly sat at their table, opening a large, black book in front of them. "Did you enjoy your meal?" she asked, to which both replied in agreement that their meals were fine. With pen poised, she then said, "That's great, so when would you like to book again?"

A similar approach is used by a successful dental surgery that only takes new patients by referral. The practice will not accept a booking unless you have been referred by another patient. You are also not allowed to be late or cancel a booking, or you will be deleted from the customer base.

So, how exclusive can you make doing business with you?

BREAK THE MOULD

You can also be unique by just being a little different from your competitors. Richard Branson created the Virgin brand by daring to be different, challenging the norm, and living on the edge. From record breaking attempts in hot air balloons to going head-to-head with British Airways, the Virgin brand was independent, demanding, and a pioneer in every new market it captured.

Who said that a bank must look after its shareholders first and its customers second, an accounting firm must provide financial and tax advice, and a lunch bar must offer pre-made lunches? Who set that mould, and why can't it be broken? Bendigo Bank, ITP (Income Tax Professionals), Airbnb, and Uber certainly believed it could, and now these are very successful businesses.

Time to roll up our sleeves again before moving to the next chapter. Follow this step-by-step guide for creating your Unique Selling Proposition.

CREATING YOUR USP

The process for creating your USP starts with a few simple questions that you'll need to answer.

1. What are you passionate about?

2. What are you best at?

3. *What is the economic driver (that is, what would you get paid by others to do)?*

Next comes the What, How, and Why of your business. American author and inspirational speaker, Simon Sinek, states: "People don't buy what you do, or even how you do it, people buy … why you do it." In essence, your USP is a summary or statement of your 'why'.

Let's begin with brainstorming some words that come to mind when you think about the business you are creating. The SWOT analysis you did in the last chapter can help – here's an example of a completed SWOT for a college.

STRENGTHS

- Small classes/personalised teaching
- Great QILT scores - outperforms others
- New team without legacy
- Graduate word of mouth
- Project based learning/real world briefs
- Classes taught by industry professionals
- Generous scholarship offering
- Boutique learning environments

WEAKNESSES

- Low brand recognition/low school engagement
- Smaller campuses/lack of services
- High domestic fees
- New team without internal knowledge
- Cost (value for money)
- Lack of global brand awareness
- Limited info to international students

OPPORTUNITIES

- Online study opportunities
- Three-day study week
- Engaging with high school market
- Growth leads to better facilities
- Flexibility of courses
- Industry internship program
- Create a clear brand position
- Post graduate course options
- Adopt a challenger brand mentality

THREATS

- Lower entry requirements from other brands
- Perception of being an 'international' college
- Lower fees from competitors
- Other providers moving in our USP
- Staff being poached by competitors
- Declining employment opportunities
- Declining domestic students to universities
- Changes to visa/immigration
- Changes to loan structures

Using the SWOT you completed and the answers to the three questions at the beginning of this workout section, write down some of the keywords used in the boxes below.

The next step is to sort out the words into three categories: What, How, and Why. Using our example of the college above, they might sort their keywords as follows...

What
Great QILT scores – New team – Industry professionals

How
Generous scholarships – Flexible course timetables – Three-day study week – Online study opportunities

Why
Project based learning/real world briefs – Small classes

The next step is to shape these into a statement that starts with the who, then the what, the how, and, finally, the why. Here is an example of how this might look…

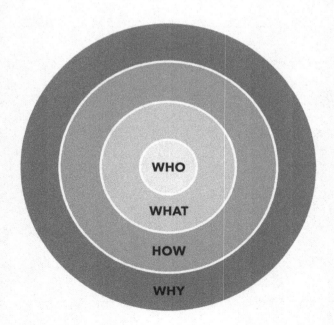

Complete the following statement for your new business.

WHO

Our business exists to serve...

WHAT

For whom we make/deliver...

....

....

....

....

....

....

....

....

....

....

....

....

....

....

....

HOW

We do this by...

WHY

At XYZ business we believe in...

Now the final step is to look at your statement and from that determine a tagline of ideally three or four words. Apple, for example, uses 'Think Differently', Nike 'Just Do It', and in the College example, it could be 'Effective Real World Learning'.

Your USP is...

....

....

....

....

....

....

....

....

....

....

....

LET'S GET
PERSONAL

Congratulations! You are halfway to creating your new business, your future, and your destiny. It is said that God created the Heavens and Earth in six days and on the seventh day, he rested – and so should you.

Now, although you can take some time to reflect, relax, and maybe even look for a reward or two, it is also the time to take a good look at yourself. In today's digital world, your 'personal branding' can be equally as important as your business branding. You are the heart and soul of the organisation, so the vibrancy, originality, and, ultimately, the success of your new business will come from you.

YOUR PERSONAL BRANDING COMES FROM THE HEART

Driven by the popularity of social media, business owners can no longer hide behind their business brands. Whatever you have done or, in some cases, not done can be instantly Googled by any prospective customer, associate, or competitor. Whenever you attend an event and smile for an innocent photograph, that image could easily and quickly end up online for the world to see. So, creating and maintaining a favourable personal brand is a vital component of your business success.

Let's take a look at the five key areas of your personal brand.

FIT FOR LIFE

In the first half of this book, you probably discovered that you are going to need a great deal of energy and passion to create, launch, manage, and grow your new business. Having a healthy body and a healthy mind will help lead you towards building a healthy business too.

Today's modern, forward thinking medical practitioners believe that if you see a doctor when you are sick, then they haven't done their job properly. Instead, you should treat your doctor like a health coach, who prepares an action plan for you to stay healthy and avoid illness. Let's face it, when you are running your own business, sick leave becomes a thing of the past. If you don't work, then you won't get paid.

Nutrition can also have a big impact on your energy levels as well as your personal appearance. Eating healthy can be difficult, especially if you are constantly on the run. Nutritionists tell us that we need over 40 different nutrients to achieve good health, and no single food source supplies them all.

Here are some simple tips to follow to stay as healthy as your growing new business:

- Eat plenty of whole grains, nuts, fruit, and vegetables
- Maintain a healthy weight
- Eat food in moderate portion sizes

- Chew your food well
- Eat on a regular basis, and try not to skip meals
- Reduce certain foods, like those with a high fat or sugar content, rather than eliminating them altogether (the reason why most diets don't last)
- Eat fresh and avoid fast food.

DRESS FOR SUCCESS

As the saying goes – "You don't get a second chance to make a good first impression." Research has shown that within 7 seconds, people will form 11 impressions of you. This is known as the 7/11 rule.[1]

But according to a study by Princeton psychologists Janine Willis and Alexander Todorov, it can take a mere tenth of a second to form an impression of a stranger from their face. Furthermore, longer exposure does not significantly alter those impressions.[2]

Whatever the timing, first impressions will be formed, and subconscious decisions will be made about you – even before you have uttered your first word!

We generally associate well presented individuals with intelligence and achievement, and, all in all, most people like to employ, do business and be associated with winners. Business is a competitive game that needs to be played with strategy and control. You need to impress, instead of depress, at meetings and presentations. Remember, 'attraction' instead of 'distraction'.

Wear fashionable but not overly trendy outfits, and choose colours that match your complexion. Similar to the branding for your business, choosing the right corporate colours will enhance your image. Invest in a session with a personal colour consultant or stylist, who can prepare for you a swatch of the colours that work best for you. Just think how easy clothes shopping will be when you have a limited selection of colours from which to choose that you know, professionally, will look good on you.

PLAN AND PREPARE

The main goal of any meeting is to listen. We have two ears and one mouth, so we really should use them in that proportion. In every meeting, you must make the other person feel important. Columnist and author, Barry Farber, writing for Entrepreneur, suggests that you ask the person you are meeting, "Do you mind if I take notes?"[3] This shows the person that you are really listening and you want to hear what they have to say. You can usually watch the effect, as they sit up taller in their seat.

Try to set an agenda for the meeting. A meeting without an agenda is like an orchestra without a conductor. An agenda sets expectations and outcomes for the meeting and keeps everyone on track.

LEARN THE ART OF COMMUNICATION

Business communication is part of corporate culture. It is the process of engaging people to listen, understand, and want to know more about you and your business. Good communication matters because, regardless of what we do, sell, or deliver, we are all ultimately in the 'people' business. As Robert Kent, former dean of Harvard Business School, said, "In business, communication is everything."

Communication is not just about the way we speak; it encompasses the way we write, our vocabulary, our body language, and our presentation skills. According to a 2004 report by the National Commission on Writing for America's Families, Schools, and Colleges, "People who cannot write and communicate clearly will not be hired."[4]

You, as a business owner, need to be able to communicate effectively at different levels with many different types of people of different ages, ethnic heritages, races, physical abilities, genders, religious beliefs, and sexual orientations. If you are not a confident speaker, then enrol in a course on public speaking to dramatically improve the way you communicate on both a personal and professional level.

MAKE YOURSELF 'SOCIAL MEDIA FRIENDLY'

In networking terms, the adage used to be, "It's not what you know, it's who you know." In today's technologically advanced world, the catchphrase has changed to, "It's not who you know, it's who knows you."

Your personal branding will be promoted through social media, whether you like it or not. With a growing, worldwide audience out there, it is vital that you create and manage your social media profiles professionally. But designing and creating your profiles is just the start. Now, the work really begins.

SETTING AND ACHIEVING GOALS

Don't be fooled by the myth, "If you build it, they will come." To create and establish your personal brand successfully, you will need to actively communicate everything you have created to others and to the world: your dreams, goals, and map of success.

Suppose you've packed the car ready for a trip. Wide, open spaces, coastal plains, and inviting country towns – you plan to experience it all. You start the car, and off you go, en route to your first stop: the Australian War Museum in Canberra. Before long, you come to an intersection and realise that your navigation app has stopped working. You stop and panic for a moment, unable to get the application working again, but then you convince yourself that it doesn't matter because you pretty much know where you are going. Many of us treat goal setting exactly the same way: we dream of where we want to go, but we don't actually have a map of how to get there.

So, let's take a moment to do a little dreaming and follow some clear steps to plan a route to get where we want to go. The route will be supported, sponsored, or driven by our new business venture.

IS THE GOAL SOMETHING YOU REALLY WANT TO ACHIEVE?

Just because a goal sounds good, it does not mean it is right for you. When setting goals, it is very important that you remember to make them consistent with your personal values. Values influence everything in our lives because we measure all of our actions against our values. For example, if you tell a lie to someone, how does this make you feel in regards to your values of honesty and respect?

So, when setting your goal, make sure it is something that you really want and not just a passing desire. To achieve your goal, you will need passion, commitment, and a great deal of energy.

WRITE YOUR GOAL DOWN IN DETAIL

By writing down your goal, you demonstrate to your mind that you are committed to achieving it. The more detail you use, the more believable it will be. If you want a new house, then write, for example "a 300-square-metre, modern home with five bedrooms, three bathrooms, a pool, and a view of the valley, on 5 acres of land." Your subconscious mind will have a detailed set of instructions to help guide you on the right path to achieving that goal. The more information you give it, the more definite the final outcome becomes.

THINK BIG, AIM HIGH!

There is a saying that goes, "Whether you think you can or whether you think you can't, you are absolutely right." Our subconscious mind believes what we tell it so if we say we can't do something, then we probably won't be able to do it.

Dare to dream a little and go for the big goals – as long as you are passionate about them and have the motivation to do whatever it takes to achieve them.

MAKE A PLAN TO ACHIEVE YOUR GOAL AND STICK TO IT

In Napoleon Hill's book, *Think and Grow Rich*, it is stated: "*Wishing* will not bring riches. But *desiring* riches with a state of mind that becomes an obsession, then planning definite ways and means to acquire riches, and backing those plans with persistence which *does not recognise failure*, will bring riches."[5]

Hill also says that before success comes in a person's life, that person will meet with a great deal of temporary defeat and perhaps even some failure.[6] Often, defeat overtakes a person, and the easiest, most logical thing for that person to do is to quit. If you are truly passionate about the goal you want to achieve, then you will do whatever it takes to get there, and you will not give up until the job is done.

READ YOUR GOAL AS THOUGH YOU HAVE ACHIEVED IT

You can trick your subconscious mind into believing that you have already achieved a goal by, first, writing down the goal in the present tense. Let's say your goal is to be a keynote speaker at an international conference. The idea is to write the goal down as if you are already there. For example, "It's 4:00 pm on Wednesday, 3 May, 2028, and I've just checked in to my suite at the five-star Ritz-Carlton in New York. The view over the Manhattan skyline is breathtaking. I have two hours now before dinner to read over my presentation for tomorrow's Global Warming Conference…" and so on.

You can bring the goal to life by describing it 'in

the moment', and, because your subconscious mind only believes what you tell it, your mind will spring into action to set a clear path to making the goal a reality.

It is also important that you set a time in which to achieve your goal so you have a definite date to aim for. Be as realistic as possible – give yourself enough time to do the necessary steps that are needed to achieve the goal, but not enough time for procrastination to set in.

BELIEVE IN YOURSELF

When you go it alone and step out into your own business, there is no boss to hide behind, no assistant to take the rap if you make a mistake. You have to stand on your own two feet and believe in yourself. If you don't believe in yourself, how can you expect others to believe in you?

The story of Colonel Harland Sanders, as described in this section, demonstrates this well because it shows how perseverance, determination, and ambition can build success.

LEARNING THE ROPES

We all have to start somewhere, and where we begin does help to shape us in the future. Harland Sanders picked up the art of cooking from an early age, and he could prepare many dishes. He worked in a variety of different jobs, such as farmhand, soldier, fireman, insurance salesman, and he even studied law.

THE PRODUCT

At 40, Harland Sanders began cooking out of a service station he was running, focusing on mastering his product: a chicken recipe like no other. As he tried and tested herbs and spices to make the perfect fried chicken, word got out, and soon there were large queues forming to taste his new recipe.

THE UNIQUE SELLING PROPOSITION (USP)

Every business needs its own USP and for Harland Sanders, it was his trademark 11 herbs and spices. As a product, his chicken sold well, and, in 1935, he was officially made an honorary Colonel in the state of Kentucky.

TURNING A CHALLENGE INTO AN OPPORTUNITY

In 1950, Colonel Sanders shut his restaurant down because of a new highway that bypassed the service station, and the Colonel was forced to retire and apply for social security. Refusing to accept his fate, he decided, at age 65, to try and franchise the only asset he had: his chicken recipe.

MARKETING DOOR-TO-DOOR

He travelled the state, from restaurant to restaurant, promoting his chicken, but most places had their own chicken on the menu and refused to sell the Colonel's. Legend has it that he actually received 1009 knock backs before he found his first customer.

Just imagine if he had quit after 100 rejections, or even 500. How many of us would have got to the 1000th "no" without thinking, *Maybe I should change my recipe?*

BUILDING THE EMPIRE, GROWING THE BRAND

Colonel Sanders' dream of franchising his chicken started to take shape, and, by 1964, he had 600 KFC franchises, with a business valued at over $2 million USD (that's equal to around $18 million USD in 2023).

In 1976, Colonel Sanders was ranked as the world's second most recognisable celebrity. So, believe in your product and, above all, believe in yourself, and you too will realise some remarkable achievements.

In Chapter 14, which will describe our last day together before you launch your new business venture, we will look at 'Getting the Balance Right'. This will be where you will align your business plan and the goals you have set down here.

So, let's now set some SMART goals together. Goals that are Specific, Measurable, Achievable, Relevant, and Time-Bound, helping to ensure that your objectives are achievable within a certain time frame.

MY SMART GOALS

We are going to create five SMART goals in this section, and, to help you work these out, let's start with the 'Wheel of Life'.[7]

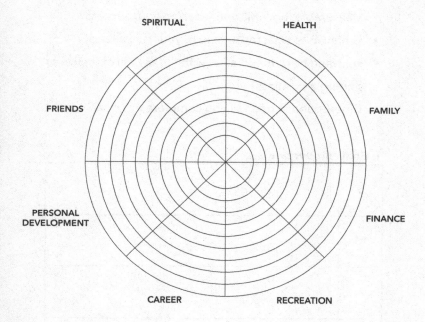

On the above wheel, plot each of the areas of your life out of ten. For example, if you feel your family life is ten out of ten and there is no room for improvement, colour in all of the levels within the 'family' quadrant.

Once you have completed your Wheel of Life, take a step back and look at how smooth or wonky your wheel is. The aim now is to select your SMART goals in order to even out the wheel so you'll have a smoother ride as you launch your new business.

Now let's begin writing your five SMART goals – complete each line by identifying…

- Specific: name the goal
- Measurable: how will you measure your success?
- Achievable: what resources do you have already?
- Relevant: how does it align with the overall objective of starting a business?
- Time-Bound: when will you complete this goal?

1. Goal number one is…

S	
M	
A	
R	
T	

2. Goal number two is...

S	
M	
A	
R	
T	

3. Goal number three is...

S	
M	
A	
R	
T	

4. Goal number four is...

S	
M	
A	
R	
T	

5. Goal number five is...

S	
M	
A	
R	
T	

TIME FOR A LITTLE CREATIVITY

With all the background work completed and the foundations laid for your new business, it's time to start building your brand.

In the previous chapter, we discussed the art of personal branding. Now, we apply the same principles to creating your business brand. The first step, however, is to understand what the term 'branding' really means. For example, do a Google search for the words 'brand terms', and you get an impressive list of over 5 billion results. In effect, you only need to consider six of these:

- **Brand promise** – your USP or the benefits you deliver to your customers that your competitors don't
- **Brand identity** – the mark/s that visually represent your brand, including your logo, stationery, and signage
- **Brand image** – the set of beliefs around what your brand stands for
- **Brand strategy** – how you advertise, market, and promote a positive perception and a desire to buy your product in your customers' minds
- **Brand positioning** – how your brand stands up against your competitors in the marketplace
- **Brand management** – maintaining consistency with your brand across different mediums and applications.

Make sure you cover all of the elements of a strong brand and don't just design a pretty logo. This is one of the best investments you'll ever make for your business.

CREATING A LOGO INSTEAD OF A 'NO GO'

Your logo is one of the most important assets to your business. Take Coca-Cola, for example. The Coca-Cola logo could be licensed or sold today for millions of dollars – and that's just the logo, not even the company.

Your logo is the pivot point of your business operations, and everything you do from here on in will be recognised and remembered by this one visual element. Your customers react and interact with it; your marketing materials feature it, and your advertising promotes it. It's not just a pretty picture. The colours chosen, the typeface selected, and the illustrations you use all blend together to create a 'feeling' for your business. Your logo creates that all-important first impression for your potential customers.

A logo should be current, so expect to 'refresh' it every three to five years. A logo that is more than five years old can look dated and somewhat disconnected from market trends. You are probably not reading this book dressed in clothes you purchased five or so years ago. Fashions and trends change, and so too should your business image so it continues to move with the times and engage with society.

In a creative, modern design, the use of colour also adds vibrancy to a brand and delivers a physiological message to your potential customers. Your logo should incorporate at least two colours and usually no more than four. These colour combinations create subliminal meanings in the minds of consumers. For example, dark blue creates a feeling of trust and authority, orange a sense of creativity, and purple a message of wealth.

In the Business Workout section at the end of this chapter, you will find a page headed 'Choosing Your Corporate Colours'. This will outline the subliminal and physiological meanings of a colour to help you select the corporate colours that best represent your business and what they stand for.

Today's digital world and modern printing methods have made full colour more affordable than ever before, so don't be scared to use brighter, more creative colours for your business identity. A word of warning though – make sure the colour chosen will work as well on a computer screen as it does on a printed letterhead or business card. Colour consistency across all mediums is vital to brand building.

Ideally, you should engage the services of a qualified graphic designer to develop your logo because this will form the foundation for your overall business brand. An initial outlay of a few thousand dollars now will turn out to be the best investment you could make in ensuring the success of your business in the future.

If you haven't the budget to engage a qualified graphic designer, then there are a few alternatives that exist online:

- **Auction sites** – Websites like www.designcrowd. com.au and www.99designs.com.au allow you to pitch your logo project to an online pool of designers and receive several concepts from which to choose. You then pay a few hundred dollars for the final selection.
- **Design your own** – Websites like www.logomaker. com allow you to choose a base template that is relevant to your industry and then customise it online, without the need to download software. When you are happy with your final design, you can purchase the logo (often for under $200).

Whatever you do, avoid creating a logo on your own computer from scratch using Microsoft Word unless you have design training. There are many logo elements that need to be considered, including font selection, type positioning, illustration choice, and so on, and they all contribute to a successful brand.

Maybe, someday, your logo could be worth millions, just like Coca-Cola's.

MAKE YOUR MARK AND PROTECT IT!

Bringing it all together – your business name, logo, and your USP (in the form of a catchy tagline) – is the basis for what is termed your 'corporate identity'. But there is one more thing that should not be missed: your trademark.

In Chapter 4, when you developed your business name, you would have conducted a search to check that the name was available and was not already protected. Trademarking your business or product name and your logo imagery is vital to your long-term growth and the protection of your market share. Imagine if, one day, years after launching your business, you receive a letter in the mail from a company with a similar name or logo to you stating that you are infringing their trademark and that you need to change your brand immediately. Worse still, what if they also seek compensation for the trademark infringement? This could cost thousands, or much more, if you decide to fight it.

You can register your trademark easily online at IP Australia's website (www.ipaustralia.gov.au/). You can choose to register just the name or the complete brand, incorporating the logo, name, and positioning statement. If you plan to take your business or product overseas, then you will also need to search for availability of your trademark in all countries where you plan to launch. You can conduct an initial search for an international trademark using the World Intellectual Property Organization's Madrid international trademark system at https://www3.wipo. int/madrid/monitor/en/.

Registering a trademark can cost as little as a few hundred dollars but could end up being worth thousands. One of the biggest assets of your business is its brand, and this can be one of the main reasons why a customer chooses you over your competitors – so make sure you protect it with a registered trademark.

IMAGE IS EVERYTHING

Your image in the marketplace determines how people respond to your brand. Creating the right first impression is vital for attracting long-term customers to your new business.

Your business image is made up of three main areas: your visual image or your logo, your sensory image, and your subliminal image. Together, these combine to produce the 'feeling' associated with doing business with your organisation. So, think about what kind of feeling you want your business to convey to your potential customers – for example, trustworthy, dynamic, modern, traditional, fast, or caring.

Your visual image, which will eventually include not only your logo but also marketing materials, signage, an online presence, and advertising, will have a colour palette, imagery, and typeface that you will select that best represents who you are. For example, if you want to deliver to customers the feeling of a 'smart, forward thinking' organisation, then your logo should be sophisticated, clean, and modern, with colours that promote creativity and professionalism.

Next comes your sensory image. This is the area in which you can really bring to life and enhance your business image. A sensory image looks at how your business communicates with the customer across all of the five common senses of sight, touch, smell, hearing, and taste. A local fashion chain, for example, may create their 'fresh' sensory package using a plasma screen in the store, showing people enjoying life in the clothes they sell (sight), convenient, brightly coloured changing rooms where customers are encouraged to try on the clothes (touch), incense or fresh flowers throughout the store (smell), background music or a water feature (sound), and chocolates, mints, or fresh fruit at the counter (taste).

Finally, there is the subliminal image. This is how you interact and communicate with the market – from the wording on your website to the way you or your staff talk to customers. It's this image that helps forge a connection and build a relationship between the customer and your brand – the hidden feeling of wanting to keep doing business with you instead of your competitors.

Why not test your business image by taking the role of the customer for a change? Put yourself in the shoes of a typical customer that you hope to attract, and measure how your business image would make you feel. Then compare the results with how your competitors might make a customer feel.

CHOOSING YOUR CORPORATE COLOURS

Choosing colours based on their subliminal meaning can help you create the right colour palette for your business. You will need to choose colours – a primary and a secondary colour, for your new logo. Look at the following colours and their meanings and use the tick box to choose your two logo colours – place the number 1 next to your primary colour choice and the number 2 next to your secondary colour.

	Orange – creativity
	Dark blue – trust, loyalty, wisdom, and intelligence
	Light blue – ideas, tranquility, and calmness
	Purple – power, nobility, luxury, and ambition
	Yellow – positivity and play, evoking happiness
	Green – growth, money, healing, and nature
	Red – love, appetite, danger, and excitement
	Black/grey – luxury, secrecy, and distinction
	White – safety, purity, and cleanliness
	Violet – royalty, mystery, glamour, and nostalgia
	Brown – earth, wood, and dependability or reliability

As you choose your colours, try them side by side to see how they look, for example, blue and orange or yellow, green and yellow, red and yellow, orange and grey, or violet and pink all can work well together.

CHOOSING YOUR FONT AND ICONOGRAPHY

Once you have your colours locked in, it is time to choose the elements of your new logo – your font or typeface and some iconography or graphic imagery.

Here is a selection of common typefaces you could choose for your logo.

Raleway	Lora	**Ultra**
Avenir	Playfair Display	Old Standard
Poppins	Garamond	*Yellowtail*
Gotham	Noto Serif	**BEBAS KAI**
Montserrat	Roboto Slab	Nunito
Source Sans	Source Serif	**BUNGEE**

If you are using a graphic designer to create your logo, then this final part won't be needed, although providing some image options that you like may help your designer to create a logo you'll love much sooner.

1. Go to https://www.gettyimages.com.au to conduct a search for relevant images.
2. In the search bar, type the word 'illustration' followed by the image you would like to find. For example, a search for 'illustration van' delivers 100+ pages of images of different types of vans, from sketches to icons and vectors.
3. You can use these for your inspiration board to share with your designer, but, as they are

copyrighted, you can't use them without purchase. If you do want to buy the image, add it to your cart and make the purchase.

FAIL TO PLAN OR PLAN TO FAIL

Your business is like a freight train, ready to leave the station and speed to its destination – but you haven't finished laying the track! In Chapter 5, you developed the 'startup business plan', which formed the blueprint for building your business. Now it's time to pick up where you left off and develop a complete business plan. That plan will be the train track that will take your business to success.

Every business needs a business plan, but it doesn't need to be complicated. In actual fact, the simpler the plan, the better. If your business plan is only five or so pages long, you will be more likely to refer to it regularly than if it is a 50 page, bound document. Like any plan, it needs to be versatile – versatile enough to adapt and adjust to keep your business on course as you enter new, unchartered waters.

YOUR RIGHT-HAND MAN

Having a business plan is like having a right-hand man: a person who acts as your chief assistant, helping and supporting you in your everyday work.

Interestingly enough, like the five fingers on your right hand, your business plan should contain just five main sections. We will now look at these five areas in more detail.

1. EXECUTIVE SUMMARY

Although this will form the start of your business plan, you should write it last. As the name suggests, it is a summary or overview of your entire business plan, and it needs to be well-written and comprehensive so people will read on. Think of this as the title and back cover of a good book – you are interested by the title of the book when you see it on the shelf, so you pick it up, turn it over, and read the back cover blurb. If you like what you read, then you purchase the book.

2. BUSINESS PROFILE

This section of your business plan reveals the driving force behind your business. If it were a fiction novel, then this would be the plot. Your profile should explain what you have in mind for the business, including a mission statement, goals, and objectives.

Just like that Apollo rocket on its mission to the moon, your business needs a mission too. Think about what your business will actually do for its customers, what it will offer the market, and why it will do everything better than its competitors.

Now put all of this into a clear statement of, generally, less than 50 words that you can follow and share with others as your business grows and develops.

The following are the three steps for creating a meaningful mission statement:

- **Test it** – A mission statement should be concise and should simply describe what your business does and for whom. Show it to your mother – if she doesn't understand it, then start again.
- **Value it** – A meaningful mission statement goes way beyond dollars and cents, so forget the money and focus on innovation and creativity. Your mission is designed for you and your business, so it should be inspiring and motivational.
- **Measure it** – Be sure to measure your mission statement against your market positioning, your customers, and your competitors.

Your mission statement is also an extension of the USP you developed back in Chapter 6. For example, let's look at Domino's Pizza's finding that customers were more interested in how quickly they could get their pizza delivered than in the price, variety, or even taste. With a USP of delivered in "30 minutes or it's free," they needed a mission statement that incorporated how they were going to meet this promise, and here it is: "Domino's Pizza is the pizza specialist who consistently delights the customer with great taste and choices in pizza with friendly, courteous team members providing prompt, safe delivery service."[1]

While the USP or brand promise is used for external marketing, the mission statement is used internally to help drive the business.

3. MARKET ENVIRONMENT

You are probably familiar with the term 'marketing'. Marketing is the process of promoting your business to acquire and retain customers. So, it goes without saying that to do marketing well, you need to understand your market.

Researching and understanding the market environment into which your business is entering will help determine not only if there is a demand for your product or service, but also what the needs of your potential customers are, what size the potential pool of customers is, and how many other businesses are offering similar products or services. The better you match your customers' needs, the more likely they will be to buy from you.

Research will also help you to determine what is happening to your market environment – is it growing, shrinking, or stagnant? This is called the 'market trend' and is vital to any new business because the market trend will have a direct impact on your future growth.

As described earlier, in the 1980s, Perth retailer Stokes Music Land focused its marketing on being the leaders in electronic organs and promoted the advertising slogan, "We'll have you playing today." Within a very short time, Stokes Music Land became known as the place to go to purchase and, ultimately, learn how to play an electronic organ.

Prior to that, the company was known as a general music retailer, offering everything from pianos to sheet music, along with other instruments and accessories. By the 1990s, however, the popularity of computers was increasing, and it wasn't long before music composing software and musical keyboard attachments were released, making it easy for people to create their own music at home.

By the mid 1990s, the popularity of electronic organs was on a steep decline, and so too were Stokes Music Land retail sales. By the time the company had realised the sharp change in the market trend and attempted to re-promote itself as a general music store, it was too late. Stokes closed the doors of all its stores in 1997.

Understanding your market environment and potential threats to it are vital to securing a successful future for your new business.

Once you have conducted your research and determined a detailed profile of your market environment, you can create your marketing strategy. Marketing strategy sounds quite scientific, but, put simply, it is how you will achieve your marketing goals when you launch your business. To create this strategy, we look at your marketing mix, or the 'four P's': product, price, place, and promotion.

- **Product (or service)** – Having the right product for your target market requires knowing what your customers need. This will determine how your product functions or your service is delivered and will also determine your product's appearance, packaging, branding, and so on.
- **Price** – You need to set the right price for your product or service while considering what the customer will be willing to pay. Take into account the profit margin you want to achieve and what your competitors are charging, as well as what discounts you may provide, financing or leasing options, and the methods of payment you will offer.
- **Place** – You need to decide where the customer can obtain your product or service. This can include point of sale: a retail shop versus an online website, a distribution channel through agents, and so on.
- **Promotion** – This involves the communication and selling of the product or service to new and existing customers, whether it be through advertising, publicity, or a direct sales team.

4. YOUR PRODUCT OR SERVICE MIX

A lot of this has been covered in Chapter 2 – 'What Am I Going to Sell?' – but you can now fine-tune and expand on your product range with the information you have gathered from your earlier market environment research.

The product mix will help your business in a number of ways. It can:

- Help to increase your market share (how much of the available work there is in your industry sector) and your turnover
- Help to limit the risk factor of having just one product line
- Help to capture and understand the needs of your customers
- Help to reinforce your brand and what your business stands for.

You will find that not all of your products or services perform at the same level in the marketplace. If you operate a car wash, for example, you may sell plenty of standard 'wash and waxes', but fewer full detailing services. Your products are, therefore, divided into the following four groups:

- **Stars** – These are the products in your product line that have high growth and deliver high profitability, like the standard car wash in the previous example.
- **Cash cows** – These are the products that have strong popularity now but have limited growth opportunities.
- **Questionable** – These are the products that have the potential to become stars or cash cows but currently have low market share. This could be the car detailing product line in the previous example.
- **Dogs** – These are the products that have both low market share and low growth potential, often being products that you have had for a while and that have somehow lost their appeal, or the market has changed. Ideally, these products should slowly be removed from your product mix.

5. THE ACTION PLAN

Now to the final section of your business plan – the all-important 'action plan'. This is where the rubber hits the road, where all that you have learned about your market environment blends with your target customers and your product mix to produce sales.

Your business action plan should include the following three main elements:

- **Marketing plan** – How are you going to get your message out to your customers and promote your business?
- **Financial plan** – How are you going to budget for your marketing spend and your cash flow forecast?
- **Time Line** – This is generally a 12-month outline of what will be happening in your business and when.

In Chapter 12, 'Taking It to the Streets', we look at a selection of effective, low-cost marketing strategies that you can include in your marketing plan and your action plan, which will be completed in Chapter 13.

THE BUSINESS PLAN

Back in Chapter 5, you created your 'startup business plan';
now it is time to develop your full business plan. Before we
begin, go back to the end of Chapter 5 and read through
the work you did for your 'startup' business plan.

Business Overview

Complete the following overview for your new business.

Vision	
Mission	
What we sell	

Your Market

Complete the following market analysis for your new business.

Target market	
Problem we are solving	
Our competitors (Three max)	
Our USP	

Your Marketing Plan

Complete the following marketing plan.

Marketing channels (for example, social, email)	
Marketing materials (for example, brochure, flyers)	
Pricing strategy (how will you charge?)	
Your referral channels	

Your Success Metrics

What are your key objectives for measuring success?

1.	
2.	
3.	

Your Key Milestones

Referring to your SMART goals that you developed earlier, create a high level road map for your new business in its first year of operation. You can set milestones like getting your tenth customer, buying a company car, reaching a turnover of $$$, your first employee, and so on.

Month 1	Business launches	9 am on X day
Month 2		
Month 3		
Month 4		
Month 5		
Month 6		
Month 7		
Month 8		
Month 9		
Month 10		
Month 11		
Month 12		

"You don't learn to walk by following rules. You learn by doing, and by falling over."

RICHARD BRANSON

YOUR
BUSINESS
STARTUP KIT

It's time to unleash a little more creativity as we take the logo you created in Chapter 8 and develop it into a complete brand.

Remember the six elements that make up a strong brand:

- **Brand promise** – your Unique Selling Proposition (USP) or the benefits you deliver to your customers that your competitors don't
- **Brand identity** – the mark/s that visually present your brand, including your logo, stationery, and signage
- **Brand image** – the set of beliefs around what your brand stands for
- **Brand strategy** – how you advertise, market, and promote in your customers' minds a positive perception and a desire to buy your product
- **Brand positioning** – how your brand stands up against your competitors in the marketplace
- **Brand management** – maintaining consistency with your brand across different mediums and applications.

You have already completed the first element, 'brand promise', with your USP developed in Chapter 6. You have made a start on your 'brand identity' with your new business logo, and 'brand image' with your 'sensory package', both developed in Chapter 8.

In this chapter, we will be looking at the remaining elements of your brand identity and brand image, and we will make a start on your brand strategy.

BUILDING A BRAND, NOT JUST A BUSINESS

So, what is a brand? Let's consider one of the world's most iconic fast-food brands: McDonald's. Is the McDonald's brand the burgers that the company sells? Or is it the process of the company's operations? Perhaps it's the golden arches of the McDonald's logo or the "I'm Lovin' It" tagline of its advertising? The brand is not any one of these − it is all of these, and much more.

Your brand is the life and soul of your business, the driver of your marketing, and the single thing your customers will identify, connect, and engage with. Using again the example of McDonald's, think for a moment about what you feel when you see the McDonald's logo on the highway. Is it just a place to buy a burger, or is it a real consumer experience? That's why, when done well, in the minds of your customers, your brand will go far deeper than a sexy logo or smart shop front.

Having a good brand also pays great dividends:
• Your customers will want to come back time and time again for the experience of dealing with you.

- You can command higher prices for your product or service because customers realise the added benefits they receive.
- You will stand out easily from your competitors and will probably deliver a far more professional first impression than most of them.
- Over time, you will add real value to your business goodwill.

Like McDonald's, with its Big Mac® and McFlurry®, you may have what are called 'sub-brands' to support your primary or 'master brand'. Your main brand acts as the umbrella brand, whereas your sub-brands are often packaged products or services supporting that core brand.

ARE YOU SINGING FROM THE SAME SONG SHEET?

Imagine a choir whose members are all singing in a different key, or a group of dancers slightly out of time with each other. These are not very pleasant to experience, and, above all, they are not at all professional. That's what your brand will look like if you don't manage it correctly – consistency is the key to building a successful brand. Wherever you travel around the world, you will always see Coca-Cola in the same shade of red and McDonald's displaying its distinctive yellow.

Let's look at where your brand will be seen, heard, or experienced, as you prepare to launch and grow your new business.

STATIONERY

One of the most common yet underappreciated forms of marketing is your business card. It is often the first connection point that potential customers have with your business. A cheap looking, flimsy card does little to create confidence and a desire to do business with you. Your brand should be displayed professionally on business cards, letterheads, invoices, and envelopes in its correct colours and on quality stock. Printing on thicker or better quality stock may only add 10 or 20 percent to the cost, but it will add 100 percent to the delivery of a positive message.

SIGNAGE

This is also an important element of branding and marketing that is often overlooked. Your signage is your 'free' marketing. Whether you have a sign on a vehicle or on the front of your building, that sign is up there for all to see 24 hours a day and seven days a week.

Promote your brand, your USP, and a point of

contact, which could either be an easy to remember 1300 number or your web address. Talk to a specialist sign company, like Signarama, to make sure your signage and livery represent the quality of your brand and deliver the right message. Remember, signage also includes your uniform and how you and your staff dress – don't let your brand down with a tattered or dirty shirt.

MARKETING COLLATERAL

What good is a quality business card and professional signage if you hand out to customers a cheap looking, ink jet printed Word document as your brochure? When a potential customer receives your brochure, a flyer, or your price list, they are ready to buy, so you really don't want to lose them at this point.

Your marketing materials should be clearly written, well designed, and should be printed professionally. Chances are you or your daughter (who's doing well in her art class at school) won't be able to do this on your own. Either engage a graphic designer and a copywriter to produce the marketing material for you or use a professional online site.

Your marketing collateral should include the following:

- **Business profile** – If you are a one-person operation, this document will be predominantly designed around your industry experience, but make sure it is written in the first person using the word 'we' instead of 'I' so you present the image of a bigger organisation. Your business profile should also include professional photography – a picture is worth a thousand words. Use a high-end digital camera or, better still, employ a commercial photographer for a few hours to capture profile shots of you and your key staff, your premises or vehicle (complete with branded livery), and your product or service, preferably in action. Remember, people like photos that include people. A shot of a cup of coffee on a table has far less impact than a shot of a couple of friends consuming coffee as they engage in enjoyable conversation. Show your product or service in its best light – ideally, being enjoyed by a customer!

- **Services menu** – There is nothing worse than spending time and effort attracting a customer to your business only to discover that they have gone somewhere else for a product or service they didn't know you offered. Your 'services menu' or 'product list' should briefly outline everything you can offer the customer. Keep it brief, easy to read, and, where possible, include pictures.

• **Testimonials** – Even if you haven't done any work for people under your new brand yet, you may have customers you have worked with personally in the past who would be more than happy to provide a testimonial. A strong and believable testimonial will help build trust with new customers and emphasise your experience and brand promise. If a client considers you to have done an outstanding job, always ask for a testimonial – what is the worst they can say?

• **Price list** – Some people will tell you not to promote your prices publicly, but your prices are what they are, and they don't get any cheaper when a customer makes contact with you. There are many ways to present a price list: you can offer discounted packages, state prices 'from', or advertise a low weekly cost. Any way you adopt, you will address the potential issue of price from the mind of the customer. If your research into your competitors has been done thoroughly, you will know if your pricing is high or low compared to others in the market. Make sure that you include the added benefits of what you offer for the price and, again, include your USP because that sets you apart from your competitors.

- **Your online presence** – Your brand needs to transfer well across all mediums, from a printed brochure through to a website. If you were going to an event and were told there would potentially be over 200 people there, you would probably buy a new outfit and make sure you looked your best, wouldn't you? Well, your online presence can be seen by a potential audience of billions! Also, unlike being one of the 200+ guests at an event, your webpage is one of 50 billion indexed through Google. So, it is important for you to get it right! With the popularity of social media as well, your online presence may include networking sites, such as Facebook, LinkedIn, and Twitter, so make sure your brand message is correctly portrayed on these platforms as well.

There will be more about websites, social media, and building your online presence in the next chapter.

CREATING YOUR BRAND PERSONALITY

Have you ever been introduced to someone who looks smart, attractive, and even desirable only to find in conversation they are boring and lifeless? It is the job of your brand to represent you so well that this disappointment is avoided. An interesting brand can pre-sell to a customer before the customer makes the purchase and can help cement an emotional attachment that will bind the customer to your business for years to come. This is called your 'brand image' or 'brand personality'.

In small business, it is often the personality of the entrepreneur that energises the brand. If you are flamboyant and humorous, then your brand will naturally follow this model. Look at the Virgin brand and how its personality follows the adventurous and often rebellious nature of its founder, Richard Branson.

By making your brand more personal, you give the customer something tangible to relate to, and that can become the single most important reason why they choose your business over a competing brand. Think about and write down some keywords that your brand will stand for and on which your business will be built.

DETERMINING YOUR BRAND STRATEGY

Now that you have your brand promise, your identity, and your image, it is time to look at joining the dots and connecting all of this to your target market. This is what is called 'brand strategy', which is a plan of attack that will, ultimately, lead to your 'marketing plan' in Chapter 12.

Back in Chapter 3, we looked at who you were going to sell to and determined the 'target market' or most probable customers for your new business. To build a brand strategy, we first need to profile your ideal customer and get inside his or her head. We need to determine:

- What newspapers or magazines they read
- What radio stations they listen to and when
- What their core values are and what is important to them right now
- Where they live, work, and socialise
- How they would traditionally find your product or service, for example, Yellow Pages or Google

This is called 'profiling', and it enables you to develop an understanding of the customer and pinpoint where you should market and promote your brand for best effect. To create the biggest impact with your marketing dollar, you need to connect with as much of your target market as you can, as often as you can – this is called 'reach and frequency'.

Now, let's get to work! It's time to build 'Your Business Startup Kit', where we will add all of the items we've discussed in this chapter so you can prepare your brand identity, brand image, and begin your brand strategy.

The final two elements of your 'business startup kit', 'brand positioning', and 'brand management' will be covered in the chapters to come.

BUSINESS STARTUP KIT

Let's start with your business stationery. In a modern, digital world, some businesses don't see the need for business cards or letterheads; however, even if you don't end up printing your stationery, it should still be designed.

Business Card	• Your name and title • Company name and logo • Phone number • Email and website address • Office address • Your services/products listed on the reverse side (optional)

Letterhead	• Company name and logo • ABN and/or ACN • Full trading name • Phone number • Email and website address • Office address
With Compliments	• Company name and logo • Phone number • Email and website address • Office address
Flyer	• Company name and logo • Phone number • Email and website address • Office address • Your USP • Products/services in detail

Next is your signage. This part should not be underestimated, as this is your free advertising, whether it's a sign on a car as you drive to your appointments or a sign on a building that is seen by passing traffic.

Vehicle Decal	• Large logo • Prominent phone number • Email or website address
Vehicle Signage	• Logo and brand colours • Prominent phone number • Email or website address
Building Signage	• Logo and USP • Website address
T-Shirts, Caps, and Uniforms	• Logo and USP

"There is one quality which one must possess to win, and that is definiteness of purpose, the knowledge of what one wants, and a burning desire to possess it."

NAPOLEON HILL

ONLINE IN
NO TIME

Wow, only four days to go until the launch of your new business!

Congratulations on the work you have done so far towards creating a successful business brand.

According to the Bank of Queensland, out of the "2.5 million small businesses in Australia an estimated 20 per cent will fail in their first year, and up to 60 per cent of start-up businesses will not survive beyond five years of launching."[1] They have found that there are 10 reasons small businesses fail, including lack of research, not having a business plan or poor marketing.[2]

The good news is, with the work you've done so far, you're likely to be in the 20 percent that will succeed.

It's now Day 11 of our two-week plan to start a business, and it is time to look at the cheapest and what some may argue is the most effective platform for growing your business: the internet. In Australia alone, as of January 2023, over 22 billion people have internet access, and they spend more than $62 billion per year on online purchases.[3]

The biggest myth for small businesses today is that they think they are too small to have a website. No matter how small you are or what industry you are in, you cannot afford to not have a presence on the web.

YOUR ADDRESS ON THE SUPERHIGHWAY

Back on Day 5, you registered your domain name. This is your virtual address on the internet, the details your customers will type into their browser to find your website. You should have also set up the 'hosting' for the domain name and your emails. This means that you are ready to broadcast your website and can now use a domain email address, like steve@spotlightcleaners. com.au.

If your email hosting package allows you to have more than one email address, you should also set up a general email account, like info@spotlightcleaners.com. au, to receive general enquiries. This not only removes the clutter from emails you may receive to your own email account, but it also creates a more professional impression of your business.

Remember, for you to receive these emails, you will need to set up your email software – for example, Microsoft Outlook, Google mail, or Apple Mail – correctly or have access to webmail. Your hosting company should be able to help you with this. Also, take a moment to set up an 'email signature'. This is the footer that will automatically be placed at the end of any emails you send. Your signature should contain your name, title, contact details, your website, and your logo.

CREATING THE PERFECT ONLINE IDENTITY

Your small business website will become the most valuable tool you have in your marketing arsenal to promote and sell your products or services. If it is too complicated, badly written, or disorganised, it will communicate negatively to the world about your business. Potential customers will be judging your business based on the look and feel of your website – that's why it must be a proud extension of your brand. There are four key areas that make for a good website:

- **Visual appeal** – Your site should be visually appealing, uncluttered, and it should offer easy navigation. Keep the communication relevant to the user and not too wordy. Remember that someone will arrive at your site looking for something, and it's your job to help them find it in no more than one or two mouse clicks.

- **Fast loading** – No-one has the time to sit facing a blank screen while your site loads. Surveys show that more than half of people will leave your site if it doesn't load in less than six seconds![4]

- **Action hooks** – The sole mission of your home page is to capture the interest of the visitor and pull them into the site. Your home page should have plenty of hooks to take the visitor to other pages, or a call to action to make contact with you.

- **Search engine friendly** – What good is a fabulous website with all of the previously mentioned features if no-one can find you? With millions of webpages on the internet in Australia, it is vital that your site can be found easily by search engines.

INVESTMENT VERSUS RETURN

Before you begin creating an online presence, you need to determine your budget and how important having a website will be to your overall marketing strategy.

If you are in the trade services industry, for example, a small website of a few pages will probably be all you will need: a home page, a list of services page, and a contact page. At the other end of the scale would be a business that predominantly offers retail trading online. In this case, the website is actually the business shopfront, so the investment will be far greater. As a guide, a website can cost anything from nothing (using a free online web builder) to $20,000 (custom designed with a full ecommerce shop).

Whatever budget you decide, make sure you cover the following important considerations:

- **Flexibility** – Online templates may save you money but are often quite limited. You may find it hard to customise the template to suit your brand colours and theme, to add your logo, or even to make changes once your website is live.

- **Build for tomorrow** – Your business will grow and expand, so your website needs to grow too. Can you easily add pages and link them to the main navigation of the site?

- **Search engine friendly** – Many online web building platforms do not deliver correctly structured or coded websites that are easily searchable on the net. You need to be able to add 'meta tags' – these are the description tags that describe your business webpage – and 'keywords'. When someone is searching for information on the web, they will visit a search engine and type in some words describing what they are looking for. The search engine then checks its database and returns a list of pages that meet the words submitted. You need to add these words or phrases into your webpage so your page comes up when the search is performed.

THE ONLINE WEB BUILDER

If you have a strong eye for design and would prefer to build the site yourself, you can use one of the many self-build platforms available on the web, such as Squarespace (www.squarespace.com) and Wix (www. wix.com). These platforms offer a step-by-step process during which you select each of the features you would like on your new website. A selection of base templates are available that allow you to change the colour combination and provide copyright-free pictures for your website. Squarespace is free to try and if you decide to use the product, you can choose a monthly or annual subscription that suits your needs.

There are also more comprehensive platforms like HubSpot. Platforms like these combine website hosting with marketing and sales hubs. Their customer relationship management (CRM) suite helps businesses do things like create content, generate leads, create conversion funnels, and improve general performance.

Before you begin building your website, you should create a plan, or 'site map'. Having a plan in place means you will know how many pages you will need and what content you will feature.

CONTENT! CONTENT! CONTENT!

Whether you opt for a DIY website or employ the services of a professional web development firm, you will still need to provide the content. What are your target customers looking for on the internet? What will keep them interested in your website? How can you convert them from prospects to customers?

Here are some interesting statistics about why people surf the net:

- A whopping 88 percent of people go online to seek education or entertainment. And now, with more than two-thirds of the world's population owning a mobile phone, it's important to be mobile-friendly too. *Note: These stats are great for your business if you ensure you have an online presence.*

- 81 percent of people go online to socialise, with 72 percentwanting to be part of a community.

- 39 percent of people go online to do business, with 31 percent seeking to shop online.

- Almost half (47 percent) go online for self-development, with about one-third (31 percent) looking specifically for self-help experts.

- 66 percent of people go online to compare prices.

- Watching movies, filling up spare time, keeping in touch with friends and family, and keeping up to date with current events and news are also massive drawcards of why people surf the web.[5]

Therefore, when you begin writing the content for your website, for each page, you should create:

- **Valuable content** – Remember, quality is more important than quantity. People are time-poor, so you need to make every word count. Create content that will provide value to others and avoid 'brag and boast' style text like, "We are the best,"

"We have the fastest," "We are the greatest," and so on. Explain how your product will make my garden greener, for example, instead of how good your fertiliser is.

- **Original content** – If you keep your content fresh and original, visitors to your site will tend to stay around longer. Remember, as stated in the previously mentioned stats, many people are surfing the web for education, entertainment, and information – so give them something original, something they haven't seen before.

- **Human content** – Imagine that the person you are addressing is standing in front of you as you write your content. If you wouldn't say it in general conversation, don't write it. For example, "XYZ Company is an FBAA accredited financial brokerage and private lender dedicated to serving our clients with the best solutions for their finance needs" sounds more like a public announcement or mission statement than a warm, inviting welcome to first-time visitors to a website.

Rather than start with a blank page, you can use AI content engines like ChatGPT or Jasper AI to help you create your content; however, it is important that you reword the computer output and personalise it into your own style. Cut and paste is not the solution in a world where the barrier to entry has dropped.

BUT WHAT'S REALLY UNDER THE BONNET?

Sir Timothy John Berners-Lee, a British engineer and computer scientist, created the first ever website, which launched in 1991. In the process, he created the publishing language of the internet: hypertext markup language, or HTML.

The web has come a long way since its inception and although HTML is still used predominantly as the code for constructing websites, most are driven by a more sophisticated 'back end' or content management system (CMS). In the mid 90s, a new dynamic programming language was released, called PHP (originally standing for personal home page, but now stands for Hypertext Preprocessor), which allowed developers to create and maintain complex, database-driven websites.

In simple terms, this is similar to buying a flash sports car – it looks good from the outside, but it is really what's under the bonnet that counts!

A CMS back end to your website allows you to manage your site via a control panel. You simply log on, access the page you want to update, make the changes, click publish, and the 'live' site changes. Many of today's platforms, like HubSpot, allow you to do so much more than just manage content. You can view activity reports, send email marketing campaigns, manage client relationships, run an ecommerce store, create a forum, or publish a blog.

If your website doesn't come with a CMS, then you will be limited in what you can change or update on your site, and, in most cases, you will need to pay a web developer every time you want to make a change.

GOING LIVE, IN... THREE, TWO, ONE

Once your website is designed and your content has been added, you will be ready to go live to the world. Before you flick the switch, however, there are a few things you need to tick off your list:

- **Social media profiles** – Your website should contain direct links to your social media profiles. Back in Chapter 7, we discussed the social media marketing platforms of LinkedIn, Facebook, and Twitter. If you haven't done so already, you will need to set up your profile with any social media services you wish to use. More about this at the end of this chapter.

- **Add your keywords** – In most cases, people will look for you online by typing keywords or a phrase into a search engine. You should make a list of 20 to 30 keywords that are likely to be used to find your site and then add these to your home page code. This can easily be done via the content management system that should be included with your website.

- **Change your DNS** – The domain name that you have registered for your business needs to be told where to point to show your new website. Domain Name System (DNS) settings direct traffic from the domain name to the website, so you will need to change these in your domain name control panel. Ask your web hosting company for more details on how to do this.

Now it is time to put all this technology to work!

'Your Online Business' workout section will provide you with a template for all of the items we've discussed in this chapter so you can prepare and build your new website, create your social media profile, and be online in no time.

YOUR ONLINE BUSINESS

The first step in creating your new business website is to design the site map. This is a plan or flow map of how many pages you will have on your site, what content they will feature, and how they will be linked.

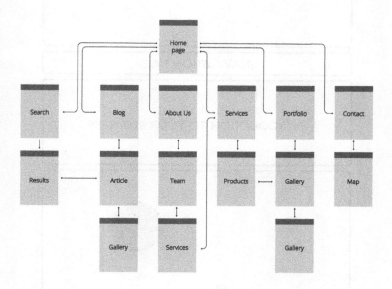

Begin with your home page at the top – this is the first page anyone will see when they visit your site. Next create the main hierarchy pages, for example: About, Products or Services, and Contact. Finally, any sub pages that will link off of the hierarchy pages; for example, you may have an 'Our People' or 'Our History' page that links off of the About page.

Next comes the layout of each page. Starting with your Home page, create a layout like this...

BANNER IMAGE

NAVIGATION BAR

INTRODUCTION TO YOUR BUSINESS

INTRODUCTION TO YOUR PRODUCTS OR SERVICES

FOOTER

Remember, each page must contain a banner header image, navigation bar, and the footer, as they form the structure of your website.

With the structure in place for each of your website pages, you can now begin creating the content. Keep the content conversational and relevant to your audience. Choose images to support your content once it is written, using Getty Images (as explained earlier) or Google images, but make sure they are copyright-free.

Now it's time to build your new website! Here are a few free platforms to help you build your website.

- Wix – Wix is a popular website builder that offers a free plan with limited features. It provides a drag-and-drop interface, making it easy to create a website without any coding skills.
- WordPress – WordPress is a website builder that offers a free plan with limited features. It is easy-to-use and comes with many templates to choose from.
- Weebly – Weebly is another popular website builder that offers a free plan with limited features. It provides a drag-and-drop interface, making it easy to create a website without any coding skills.
- Google My Business – Google My Business allows you to create a simple website for free. This option is best for small businesses that want a basic website with their contact information and business hours.

- Shopify – If you're looking to create an online store, Shopify offers a free plan with limited features. It provides a drag-and-drop interface and many templates to choose from.
- HubSpot CMS Hub – The platform is available for free, with added functionality in premium editions. CMS Hub can be connected to HubSpot's other platforms like Marketing, Sales, and Service Hubs as your business grows.

Once your website is complete, make sure that you connect your domain name (www.xyzbusiness.com.au) so customers can find you on the web.

The final step is to set up and then link your social media channels. Choose at least one social channel you will commit to, Facebook, Instagram, YouTube, LinkedIn, Twitter, or even TikTok. Create a business user account on the platform and follow the prompts to set up your page.

Now link your social media page to your website home page and contact page, asking people to like and follow you.

**TAKING
IT TO THE
STREETS!**

When the ancient Greek scholar, Archimedes, stepped into his bathtub and noted the change in the water level, he suddenly understood that the volume of water displaced must be equal to the volume of the part of his body that was submerged. He then celebrated his find by running through the streets naked shouting, "Eureka!" meaning, "I have it!"

Now, although you may not feel as motivated as Archimedes to launch your new business to the masses, in this chapter, we will be looking at a selection of effective, low-cost marketing strategies – for all of which you can keep your clothes on. These will form the foundation of your marketing plan and then your 'action plan' that will be created in the next chapter.

To begin, we need to first understand what the term 'marketing' really means. So, let's look at marketing in simple, dating terms:

- Suppose you see an attractive person at a function. You approach them and say, "I am very rich. Would you like to have dinner with me?" That's **direct marketing!**
- Or, perhaps, you might approach the same person and say, "I am very rich. Would you like to have dinner with me?" They may give you a filthy look, turn, and walk away. That's **customer feedback!**
- Or, one of your friends may approach the person and, pointing at you, say, "My friend is very rich

– you should have dinner with them." That's **advertising!**

- Or, you go up to the person, get their phone number, and call the next day to say, "Hi, I'm very rich – will you have dinner with me?" That's **telemarketing!**

- Or, you get up and straighten your attire, walk up to the person, pour them a drink, then politely ask them to dinner. That's **public relations!**

- Or, finally, the attractive person may walk up to you and say, "You are very rich – will you have dinner with me?" Now, that's **brand recognition!**

We should all strive for brand recognition in our businesses, but, to do this, especially when we are launching a business for the very first time, we need to keep our target market at the front of our minds.

An interesting fact is that brands that continued to advertise throughout the Second World War eventually became the market leaders in their fields when the war was over.[1] As summed up by Henry Ford, "Stopping advertising to save money is like stopping your watch to save time."

So, in the next section, let's explore five creative, low-cost strategies for marketing your new business and building your brand.

STRATEGIES FOR MARKETING YOUR NEW BUSINESS AND BUILDING YOUR BRAND

1. Stand out from your competitors

It is important to always remain true to your brand. Branding consistency can increase revenue by up to 23 percent because customers want brand consistency, no matter where or how they interact with your business.[2]

Leading global brands, like Coca-Cola, remain true to their brand. Wherever you go in the world, Coke generally tastes the same, and the branding remains consistent. As of February 2023, Coca-Cola was worth over $250 billion.[3]

To remain true to your brand, you need to remember what business you are in. We are all, in fact, in the same business, and that's the 'problem-solving' business.

Customers today, as they always have, buy on emotion. We need to identify what that emotion is and then become the necessary cure to their headache. You should always strive to continually educate your customers and prospects to understand, appreciate, and desire the benefit of the product or service you sell over that of your competitors.

Focus on and promote your Unique Selling Proposition and make sure everyone knows about it. Make your USP believable and, above all, measurable.

2. Double your exposure

It's amazing but true that simple and small changes to traditional marketing methods can bring about big results. For starters, you should consider printing two-sided letterheads or business cards. It doesn't double your cost – in most cases, it will only add about 25 percent more to print on both sides as opposed to printing on just one. You can use the reverse side to outline your key products or services, which will help with cross sell – or you could promote your USP.

3. Tell your customers that it is 'crab season'

Most of us love crabs. But how many of us put a big, red circle on the calendar to remind us when the crab season starts? It's the same with your new business – tell your customers when it is your business' equivalent of 'crab season' and that it is the time to buy. For example, if you are selling a winter product, like heaters or gutter cleaning, start your promotion in autumn telling customers to prepare now and buy today.

4. Increase your customer base with half the budget

Find other businesses that share the same target market as you but aren't a competitor – for example, if you are a menswear store, then find a fitness club and offer to swap newsletter articles or promotions. Make sure the databases of the two businesses match up in numbers.

It's no good approaching someone who has 2000 on their database if you only have 100 – make it a win-win situation at all times.

5. Upsell your quotes!

When you do a quote or proposal for a customer, include what the client has asked for and then add some options that they might like to consider. You'll be amazed how often they will take these up.

Amazon does this well by offering free delivery if you buy another book with your original purchase or promoting other books that people have purchased with the same theme or by the same author.

THE POWER OF THE PACKAGE

People love packages. They make it easier for people to understand the product or service offering, and they present a real feeling of value. Look at the products or services you sell and group what you offer into three easy packages: bronze, silver, and gold.

When someone is shopping around for a product or service, they will generally try to get three quotes, which is why you should offer only three packages. If you offer any more than three packages, there is the potential to confuse the customer with too much choice.

Within your packages, try to add savings or at least

reduce the cost to the lowest common denominator. For example, instead of $1500 up-front, promote $600 per month for three months (and make a bit extra too).

You will find that most people will pick the silver or 'middle' package, so they don't appear too cheap, and they believe they are getting a better deal than they would if they chose the premium, gold package.

The main thing with packages is that they help you start the sales process, and they get the issue of price out of the way at the beginning.

HOW BEING A LITTLE CREATIVE SAVED ONE BUSINESS $500,000

Back in the early 1980s, AFL came to Sydney, and the state's new team, the Sydney Swans, was born. Sydney, though, was a Rugby town, and the future of the Sydney AFL team depended on getting people to the games.

The club identified that the under-18s market was their target because these teenagers would represent the future as they grew up, got married, and had children of their own. They did some market research and found that 'music' was the common denominator or motivator for young people at the time.

They went to a top advertising agency that presented them with a campaign proposal that they believed would reach around 30 percent of under 18s, but it would take three years and would cost at least $500,000.

The club didn't want only 30 percent – they needed action now and had little money. So, they got creative and took headshots of all the players to schools and colleges throughout Sydney with one question: "Who is our sexiest player?" In the end, there was one clear winner – Warwick Capper.

Capper recorded a song, 'I Only Take What's Mine', made a music video, and wore white boots instead of the usual black and shorts two sizes too small for him so he stood out on the field. His song was played at discos and on radio, and the music video was played on television. Publicity swelled around this singing footballer. After just eight weeks, the majority of under 18s had been reached, and the cost of the whole campaign was… nil! A profit was actually made from the sale of the records.

Sydney Football Club then pioneered a new initiative. They actively created marketing campaigns towards attracting women to their games. By the end of 1986, they had more than double the number of female members of their closest rival.[4]

More recently, Tourism Queensland thought outside of the box with their 2009 "Best Job in The World" social media campaign, which advertised an island caretaker's position, offering payment of $150,000 for someone to live six months rent-free on the Great Barrier Reef.

The results were phenomenal. Thirty-five thousand

people applied from over 200 countries around the globe, and the website attracted over 50 million hits – and this was all about just one brand![5]

ADVERTISING ON A SHOESTRING BUDGET

It would be nice to have the advertising budget of a big brand like Coca-Cola, but, for most of us, every advertising dollar we spend has to produce a return.

When it comes to creating an advertising campaign to launch your new business, the first thing you must do is identify your target market. Way back in Chapter 3, we looked at 'Who Am I Going to Sell to?', and this determined our target market. If you don't know your target market or 'most probable customer', then you could waste thousands of dollars advertising to the masses, many of whom aren't interested or don't even need your product or service. To avoid this, you will be creating a 'targeted' advertising campaign that is designed to reach only those customers that are relevant to your business.

The following are some key, low-cost strategies that you should consider for your advertising 'launch' campaign.

DIRECT MAIL

Direct marketing via the letterbox, whether it be to businesses or households, has been around for decades. However, in today's over-cluttered, junk-mail-heavy world, the strategy has become more of a communication invasion than an informative sales tool. To help your own direct mail campaign cut through the overload of promotional material, catalogues, brochures, and free samples we are bombarded with every day, you need to be a little creative.

You will either need to purchase a database, build it from scratch, or use a mailing house to distribute your campaign. Nowadays, you can purchase a targeted database that is tailored to industry, business size, location, and number of employees from around $1 per name.

When designing your promotional material for direct mail, try to think outside of the square – include a product sample, send a glossy postcard instead of a cheap flyer, or at least make it bright and colourful so it jumps out of the letterbox.

Believe it or not, there are a lot of people who actually love receiving junk mail. Make sure your marketing message includes some interesting information about your product or service and a "to the home or business owner" exclusive offer.

Finally, remember that direct mail generally achieves a take-up rate, if you are lucky, of only 1 to

3 percent, but this improves substantially when you follow up with a telemarketing campaign. By using a current and correctly populated database, you should have both 'opt-in' mailing and phone data for all of your prospects. Wait a few days after sending out your marketing piece and then call to follow up each contact.

PUBLIC RELATIONS (PR) AND MEDIA RELEASES

We live, well and truly, in the 'digital age', where information is everywhere and anywhere. This increase in communication delivery platforms, from the World Wide Web to multichannel television channels and digital radio, has created a growing need for content.

In today's world, as Bill Gates famously said, "Content is king" – and not just any content, either. Audiences are better informed, better educated, and more technically competent than ever before, demanding specialised, reliable content – and this is where you come in. Whatever business you are in, you are a specialist in your own field, and the idea is to promote this via targeted articles, media releases, and blog posts. Your stories need to be topical and newsworthy – think about the reader and what they would want to get from the article you have written. Avoid any form of 'sell' in your copy because this will only discredit your article and put people off. People like to read unbiased 'editorial' rather than sponsored 'advertorial'.

You could write articles providing tips or do-it-yourself steps. For example, a plumber may write a series of articles entitled "Five water saving ideas for your home" or "How to change a tap washer in seconds." It is important that the headline for each of your articles is an attention grabber that will attract the reader and explain the content in as few words as possible.

Once you have written a few articles, start submitting them to online publications, mainstream media, local newspapers, and radio stations. For all media outlets, you should be able to locate the contact details for the editor or producer of the publication or the show you are targeting through a simple online search.

TRADE SHOWS AND EXPOS

Targeted trade shows can be an excellent platform for launching a business and building a database in a matter of days. Do some research on what events are happening both in your industry and in your local area, using your local newspaper, the Chamber of Commerce, your shire council, website directories like True Local, and, of course, Google.

Renting a stand at the more popular trade shows and expos may prove expensive; however, there are usually opportunities to co-host, sponsor, or be involved in other ways. Make sure you have plenty of promotional materials to hand out to interested people and that your stand is bright, colourful, and professional. Remember, first impressions count for everything. After the show, make sure you follow up every lead or contact with a phone call within a few days.

Run a competition to be drawn on the last day of the show and ask people to enter by placing their business cards in a bowl, or offer an exclusive 'show special'. Whatever you do, make sure you don't just hand out brochures all day and you actually obtain contact details for everyone who visits your stand.

ONLINE MARKETING

Globally, Google processes over 99,000 searches every single second.[6] This makes more than 8.5 billion searches a day.[7] Of these, Australians perform about 250,000–300,000 Google searches each day.

According to Statista, active internet users aged between 35 and 44 spend an average of over 150 hours online each month.[8]

What if some of that web surfing was coming your way?

Google itself has come a long way in enabling local businesses to target just their local area or industry-specific market instead of trying to compete on a global stage. Google Ads allows you, as a business, to create an advertisement, choose the keywords that you think people would use to search for your business, select the area or criteria in which you would like your advertisement to be shown, nominate how much you want to spend per lead, and choose your campaign period. This is a simple and effective process that can be set up and running in just a few hours, but, more importantly, it can be monitored, adjusted, and stopped at any time. It is also quite a unique advertising model in which you only pay when someone actually clicks through from your advertisement to your website. Imagine if the television industry offered to run your advertisement for free and only charged you when someone picked up the phone and called you?

To make your online Google Ads campaign more effective, follow three simple steps.

- **Avoid popular keywords** – Google Ads works on a bidding system, so the more popular the keyword or phrase, the more you will need to pay to achieve a top five ranking on the page. If you make your keywords more specific, you will achieve a higher ranking at a much lower 'click-through' cost. Therefore, instead of, say, bidding for a popular search word like 'home sales', if you have a real estate business, try keyword phrases like 'home builders Annangrove, Sydney' or 'realty specialist for first home buyers'.

- **Set up a landing page** – When someone clicks on your advertisement, they need to be directed to a specific page on your website and not just your home page. Create a specific page just for your campaign that gives more information on what your advertisement is promoting and contains a call to action form that can be completed and sent to you to secure the offer, make a booking, or obtain more information.

- **Monitor, measure, and manage** – Your Google Ads campaign should be a working canvas that you constantly tweak and adjust until you have created your masterpiece. Try different advertisements, add keywords, and delete the ones that aren't performing, change your offer, and keep tracking the results.

NETWORKING

Storytelling is the oldest form of communication and involves one person telling others about something, whether it is a real event or something made up. From these beginnings comes the art of 'word-of-mouth advertising'. In today's digital age, this has further developed into 'viral marketing' in which messages are enhanced by video clips, interactive games, ebooks, branded software, and social networking platforms.

Business networking is about building strong, lasting

relationships with other like-minded business owners who may then refer you to potential customers that they feel could benefit from your product or service. Whether it be attending an event, joining a business group, or connecting online, there is a definite art to successful networking, and some find it easier than others to master.

Back in Chapter 3, we looked at setting up your 'network' by joining groups like your local chamber of commerce and business networking groups, as well as setting up online network platforms, such as LinkedIn and Twitter.

So, now let's look at how we use networking to create the best word-of-mouth advertising for your business.

Perfecting your elevator pitch – Imagine you are in a lift with a potential customer who has just asked you the question, "So, what do you do?" Your answer, known as the 'elevator pitch', should sum up what you do in around 30 seconds, with enough information to engage the prospect without putting them off with any sales talk. You should know this pitch off the top of your head and be able to express it with passion and conviction so people will get excited by it too. Start by writing down a few paragraphs about what you do, why you do it so well, and why people need it, then start condensing that down to a 30-second read. Test it on your friends, family, and close business associates to see if they get excited by it and want to know more.

Here's an example:

As the founder of Me.Inc, I work with hundreds of small business owners to help them easily create proposals that generate sales. Do you agree, one of the biggest time wasters in running a business can be preparing countless proposals? Imagine if this whole process can be completed in just a few minutes with a click of the mouse? Would you like to know how we do it?

Know what you want to achieve – Nothing is more offensive at a business networking event than a card swapping frenzy or hard sales pitch. Networking is all about building relationships first and doing business second. When you attend an event or join a group, have a clear objective of what you want to achieve, who you want to meet, and with whom you want to ultimately connect.

Don't be afraid to network with your competitors either. For you to perfect your USP, you need to understand what your competitors do and how they do it. You will find that your competitors are a lot less 'competitive' in a relaxed 'after-five' environment.

Driving the lead to a sale – At a typical networking event, you want to aim to meet at least ten new people. Even if these people do not match the demographic profile of your ideal customer, they have a network of people to whom they can refer you. Whoever you meet, the important thing is to follow up the next day with a quick phone call, an email, or even a personally written 'thank you' card. This shows that meeting with them at the event meant something to you and reminds them of who you are and your contact details, opening the door for further communication.

Learn how to act – Whether you are a naturally bubbly person with a vibrant personality and a great sense of humour or not, you need to present a positive persona. You are the figurehead of your business and whatever people see in you, they will automatically associate with your business. There are many short courses you can do through TAFE, the National Institute of Dramatic Art (NIDA), or other institutions that will teach you how to present one on one or in public – to a small group or to a national media audience.

Effective networking can be an inexpensive way of building your brand, lifting your profile, and engaging new customers.

YOUR MARKETING ACTION PLAN

Back in Chapter 9, you began creating your marketing plan with the following:

- Marketing channels (for example, social, email)
- Marketing materials (for example, brochure/ flyers)
- Pricing strategy (how will you charge?)
- Your referral channels.

Now it is time to build that into your Marketing Action Plan so you can hit the ground running as soon as your business is launched.

YOUR ELEVATOR PITCH

Here is an example of an elevator pitch for Airbnb:

> *Most tourists booking online care about price – and hotels are one of the highest costs for when traveling...*
>
> *We have created a platform that connects travelers with locals, letting them rent our rooms, or even entire places. Travelers save money, and locals can monetise their empty rooms – we just take a 10% commission.*
>
> *How does that sound?*

Now it's your turn…

YOUR MARKETING CHANNELS

One of the biggest mistakes startup businesses make is trying to be everywhere at once. Back in Chapter 5, you selected which of the following marketing activities you were going to include in your Marketing Action Plan:

- Networking
- Social media (LinkedIn, Facebook, and so on)
- Paid media (Google AdWords etc)
- Local newspaper advertising
- Sponsorship (local footy club, and so on).

NETWORKING

Start by looking at networking groups in your local area as well as your specific area of business. Visit the website of each group and begin by attending one of their events as a guest. Complete the following...

Group Name	Website/Phone	Next Event
Chamber of Commerce		
Local BNI Chapter		
Local Rotary Club		
Shire Council Local Business Events		
Industry Meet-ups (Eventbrite)		

SOCIAL MEDIA

Before you choose your social media channels, you need to consider which ones your target customers are more likely to use. For most startup businesses, the following channels are suggested…

Facebook	<ul><li>Set up a company page.</li><li>From the Pages section, click Create New Page.</li><li>Add your page name and category.</li><li>Add your page's bio and click Create.</li><li>Add information, such as contact, location, and hours, and click Next.</li><li>Add profile and cover photos, edit the action button, and click Next.</li></ul>
LinkedIn	<ul><li>Set up a company page.</li><li>Click the Work icon in the upper-right corner of your LinkedIn home page.</li><li>Scroll down and click Create a Company Page.</li><li>Select the page type.</li><li>Enter your page identity, business details, and profile details.</li></ul>
YouTube	<ul><li>Sign in to YouTube on a computer or the mobile site.</li><li>Go to your channel list.</li><li>Choose to create a new channel or use an existing Brand Account.</li><li>Fill out the details to name your new channel.</li><li>Upload your video content.</li></ul>

PAID MEDIA

There are a number of simple ways to get started with paid media but before you start, determine your 'lifetime' budget that you will be allocating to this channel.

Boosting a Post

When you put up a post on any of your social media channels, you can 'boost' that post so you can attract more views than just the followers of your channel. Simply find the post you want to boost, then click the 'boost' button in the lower-right corner. Fill out the ad targeting, link, and budget options and you're good to go.

Paid Social

Each of the social media channels you have selected offer the option to run ad campaigns across their network. You can use platforms like Hootsuite to manage your paid and organic content on Facebook, Instagram, and LinkedIn. Alternatively, you run campaigns directly within your social media platform of choice and manage it there. For LinkedIn, for example, click on 'For Business' and then the 'Advertise' icon.

Paid Search

Google handles around 300,000 searches per day in Australia, and you can bid for 'sponsored' ads that appear at the top of a specific search. Targeting is the key here so you don't waste your budget on irrelevant audiences. Google offers specific targeting, such as:

- Affinity segments: Reach users based on what they're passionate about and their habits and interests.
- Custom segments: Custom segments help you reach your ideal audience by entering relevant keywords, URLs, and apps.
- Detailed demographics: Reach users based on long-term life facts.
- Life events: Reach users when they're in the midst of important life milestones.
- In-market: Reach users based on their recent purchase intent.
- Your data segments: Reach users that have interacted with your business.
- Website and app visitors: Reach people who have visited either your website or your apps.
- Customer match: Reach your existing customers based on your CRM data.
- Similar segments: Reach new users with similar interests to your website visitors or existing customers.

Setting up a Google Ads account is easy. Make sure you're logged in to your Google account (or create a new one), then go to ads.google.com. Once you've chosen your account, you'll be shown the first step for setting up a new campaign.

LOCAL NEWSPAPER ADVERTISING

Community newspapers are consolidating in a lot of states, so search online for your local community paper. You will have the option of advertising in the printed edition as well as the digital version. You can advertise in the main paper or in the classifieds under Trades and Services.

Consider also local community radio where advertising can be quite cost effective, maybe as little as a few hundred dollars a week.

SPONSORSHIP

Your local community is generally where your first customers will come from, so it makes sense to sponsor events, sporting teams, or organisations in your region. You could offer to provide a prize for a raffle at a local charity event or provide shirts (with your logo) for the local footy team.

BUILDING
YOUR
EMPIRE

We are only a couple of days away from launching your new business, and, once that happens, if you've done everything right, like riding an exciting rollercoaster, you'll have to hang on tight and enjoy the ride! Just like a rocket heading to the Moon, you will have the power to lift off, and you will have a good idea of where you are heading – but have you planned the journey?

For the rocket, it must accelerate from 0 to over 40,000 kilometres per hour to escape the Earth's gravitational pull. The rocket then goes through a series of burn stages that each take it to a higher velocity and altitude. Your business is much the same, except for the fact that you'll be staying on Earth – unless you are part of Sir Richard Branson's Virgin Galactic, the world's first commercial spaceline.

As your business grows and expands, you will need to address a number of key areas. Remember that as soon as you open the doors, the odds are stacked against you. Roughly a quarter of new businesses fail in the first year and almost half fail within four years.[1] Clearly, a significant percentage of businesses do fail, and many do so due to the impact of a few key factors that, if not avoided, can cause the business to slow or, worse still, sink in the perilous waters of the entrepreneurial sea. In this chapter, we will look at these key factors and how you can avoid or manage them as your business grows.

CASH IS KING

One of the most common and often fatal mistakes of any startup business is lack of capital. The excitement and passion of starting a business can cloud the judgement of a business owner. It is too easy to underestimate how much money will be needed to start and operate the business in its early days, and this can combine with unrealistic expectations for incoming revenue. The compounding effect of these two mistakes can have shocking results for the business at its most vulnerable stage.

To get a snapshot of how much capital you really need to start up your business, use a spreadsheet or one of the business calculators available online, like the one found at www.businessknowhow.com/startup.

If you think of your business as being like the human body, then 'cash flow' is the 'blood flow' of your operations – without it, everything else will grind to a halt. Even if you have enough capital to start your business, it is vital that you monitor cash flow regularly. You must make sure invoicing goes out on time, accounts are followed up for payment, expenses are kept in control, and you plan for the future.

Having a 'slush' or 'contingency' fund in which you regularly save money for use in case of emergency will enable you to budget for the future to finance such factors as machinery breakdowns, technology upgrades, and outsourcing fees.

TIME MANAGEMENT

When you are running a business, your biggest enemy is time. No matter how organised you are, there will always only be 24 hours in a day – all you can do is manage yourself effectively to make the best use of the time you have. As a small business owner, you will have many hats to wear: account manager, sales director, IT manager, marketing executive, general manager, and right back down to the employee if you are a sole operator. The following are four tips for better time management:

- **Prioritise** – One of the biggest time thieves of all is procrastination, especially when you have a lot to do and no time at all to get it all done. Bring back the basic 'to-do' list and set up your priorities for the day. This will allow your mind to focus on the most important outcomes and actions and is a wise investment of your time.

- **Balance your time** – There is nothing worse than expending your time somewhere, knowing that you should really be somewhere else. There is a little tool we looked at back on Day 7, called 'The Wheel of Life', that basically measures all key areas of your life, including family, health, career, relationships, spirituality, and relaxation. If the balance is wrong across these areas of your life, your wheel will be uneven, and you'll be in for a very bumpy ride.

- **Manage time wasters** – The biggest time wasters in business are telephone interruptions, meetings, unplanned visitors, and unexpected crises. Manage telephone interruptions by turning your phone off before 10:00 am each day or by using a telephone answering service so a receptionist can screen your calls. Keep meetings to a minimum and always prepare an agenda to help keep everyone on track. For unplanned visitors, the trick is not to make them feel comfortable – get up from your desk and meet them at the door or advise them that you only have a few minutes before your next meeting is scheduled. Finally, when it comes to unexpected crises, you need to have contingency plans in place. For example, have an old printer in the office should your main printer break down, have a spare mobile or laptop in case your main one is lost or stolen, and make sure you regularly back up all of your data.

- **Measure results** – Every time you commit to something, ask yourself if doing whatever it is will bring you closer to your goals or move you off track. The only way to know if your efforts in the area of time management are working is to constantly measure the results. Your schedule will continually need to be adjusted and fine-tuned to make sure you remain productive.

CREATING LEVERAGE

If you really want your business to grow and, more importantly, operate effectively some day without you even being there, you will need to understand the power of leverage. The best form of leverage is where you can 'clip the ticket' on a service or product you own that sells itself. Every time someone buys it or uses it, you make money without doing any physical work. You could, for example, create this form of leverage in your business by developing and selling a training video on how to use your product, or by having your product packaged and sold online or by sales agents.

The next best level of leverage is people. When you start out, you will be filling all roles within your organisation, but, as you grow, you can employ people to take on some of those roles, or you can even outsource some of them. There are a number of ways you can look at hiring people into your business:

- **Recruitment agency** – An agency acts on your behalf and searches for the right candidate to fill a vacancy. The agency will search its existing database, advertise the position, and review applications before presenting you with a shortlist of candidates. Fees for this service vary but often equate to around 10 percent of the annual salary of the position.

• **Online recruiting** – Growing in popularity, online recruiting involves posting the job vacancy on online platforms like Seek (www.seek.com.au). The sophistication of these platforms means you can advertise in a matter of minutes and start receiving applications almost immediately. The cost is just a few hundred dollars, and you will need to do all of the reviewing and interviewing of candidates yourself.

• **Contracting** – Probably one of the safest options, and this involves you contracting a person to come in and provide the resources you need. If things don't work out, the contract can be terminated. You also won't need to worry about employee-related expenses, like holiday leave, superannuation, or PAYG. However, most contractors do command a higher hourly rate than that of an employee to cover their own taxes and added expenses.

• **Outsourcing** – In some cases, your office may be too small to employ people directly, in which case outsourcing becomes an attractive option.

Administrative duties, such as bookkeeping and debt collection, are tasks that are easily outsourced. However, there is a growing popularity for outsourcing sales, marketing, and human resources activities as well. You can choose to outsource to a local company or an overseas organisation, where rates can be quite attractive.

KEEPING UP WITH TOMORROW

We live in the digital age, and our world is filled with gadgets, devices, and all things technological. If you think keeping up with today is hard enough, it's only going to get worse as we become more and more reliant on technology – especially for communication. For example, just look at Apple, which has cornered the market of lifestyle technology with products like the iPhone and iPad. No sooner had Apple introduced the first iPad when, within 12 months, the iPad 2 hit the market. The value of owning technology is diminishing rapidly – as soon as you buy something, it becomes obsolete and superseded by a faster, slimmer model.

Whatever business you are in, you will be reliant on technology to a degree. If you're not, you are probably missing out on tools and applications that will make your business run faster, smarter, and more efficiently. Let's take a quick look at some of the technology trends on the horizon that you may want to consider as your business grows:

- **Rent it, don't buy it** – Many of the leading vendors offer a lease of new technology equipment instead of an outright purchase. Independent companies like Technocorp provide access to a huge range of technology equipment from the world's top brands, where you rent either a new or preloved computer for a minimum of six months, with the option to purchase it after just a day.

  Mainstream retailers like Harvey Norman offer up to 60 months interest free or 24 months on Apple products with no deposit. This can make it easier for a business to purchase new equipment and pay for it gradually each month.

- **Cloud computing** – Data storage can become a problem for a growing business, with the need to store day-to-day transactions, associated files, email data, and ongoing backups. Cloud computing – kind of like having a giant filing cabinet in the sky – allows you to store and access your data from anywhere in the world where you have internet access. As the world becomes more remote, this option provides not only an excellent and convenient solution for a growing business but also a cost-effective alternative to having in-house computer servers and backup drives.

• **Your co-working office** – The virtual office concept allows you to have the full functionality of a working office but on an 'as needed' basis. One of the leaders in the field, Servcorp, offers a network of offices all over the world that can be accessed for a few hundred dollars per month. Each location, from New York to London to Hong Kong, comes with a reception team, smart office suite, phone and email, access to a boardroom, and a high-profile street address. There are also new online services springing up that can manage your appointments, your travel arrangements, and even your gift giving.

• **Staying connected** – Communications technology is moving ahead in leaps and bounds, and it is vital that your business keeps up with it too. There are smart business apps for your smartphone that let you scan business cards straight into your contacts, and software that can actually monitor what people are saying about your brand online anywhere in the world and in real time. With so many devices at our fingertips, it is important that you have them all connected, or 'synced'. Apple's iCloud, for example, allows you to make an appointment on your iPhone that will then automatically update on all linked devices as soon as you switch them on. Talk to your communications provider about all of the latest products on the market that suit your business and plan to update at least every two years.

YOU DON'T KNOW WHAT YOU DON'T KNOW

When you decided to start your new business, you probably either had a great idea, found a new product to market, or you worked for someone else and felt you could make it on your own. Whatever the motivation, you will find that, as your business grows, you will need skill sets that you don't have. It's not just about doing a good job for your customers; a business owner needs to wear many hats.

As your business develops and expands, your time will become the commodity that you value most. Whether you have or learn the skill set needed for all areas of your business operations, there will come a time when outsourcing makes both real sense and real cents.

Something that may take you hours to accomplish could take a specialist a fraction of the time. Not only will you get the job done more professionally than doing it yourself, but it will be done quicker, and you will be free to spend your time on more productive tasks for the business.

For example, let's look at invoicing, something every business needs to do, week in, week out. Depending on the size of your business and the number of clients or projects you have, this task could take from one hour to half a day every week. In Chapter 2, we determined what you were going to charge for your time and expertise – let's say that equates to $110 an hour. Your invoicing task each week then, assuming you have acquired the base financial skill set needed and have a good working knowledge of accounting software like MYOB, would equate to an investment of between $110 and $440 per week. On the other hand, you could employ a bookkeeper for around $60 per hour, who would do the work in at least half the time but most probably even less. This one simple change saves you $50 per hour on what you are worth and means you are now free to charge out the time you were going to spend on the task.

Around six months into your new business, take a 'reality check' and document for two weeks everything you do, from when you get up to when you go to bed. At the end of the two weeks, categorise your work into income-producing (when you are actually doing work for a customer), income-generating (like sales calls and quotes), administrative (like invoicing), and so on. From this report, you will be able to see the percentage of your time that is actually spent earning money for your business and the areas that potentially could be outsourced so you can add more income-producing time to your week.

CREATING YOUR MASTERMIND GROUP

Another way to tap into the expertise of others and increase your knowledge base is to create a mastermind group. This group of close advisors will act like your virtual board to help steer you and your business through the obstacles ahead. All large companies, especially publicly listed organisations, operate with a board who appoint a chief executive officer to run the day-to-day operations and, ultimately, control the finances and direction of the business. Being a small business operator can be a lonely journey, especially if you have never done it before, so having a mastermind group can give you the peace of mind that others are there for you to help keep you on track.

A mastermind group can be set up in a number of ways:

- A group of friends, peers, or associates that provides a variety of skill sets and experience
- Local businesses that are members of the same

organisation, like a chamber of commerce, and meet regularly to discuss each other's businesses

- A business mentor, someone you look up to, who has done the hard yards and has already created a successful business
- A business coach who you work with weekly, fortnightly, or monthly to achieve your goals, both personally and in business.

This book, for example, probably would not have been written if it were not for my business coach, Therese Wales. Running a successful branding and communications agency in Sydney and Perth was easily filling up my week, leaving little time for me to 'work on the business' instead of always working 'in' it. Therese was able to understand how I worked, help me prioritise my time and commitments, and then, ultimately, find me a day per week to write a book. Whatever your goals – maybe you don't even know what they are yet – a business coach can help you achieve them by keeping you focused and accountable.

READY, SET, GO!

So, with just one day left before you swing open the doors, start the engine, or turn on the lights to your exciting new business, it's time to begin the framework for your 'action plan': where you are now, where you want to be, and how you are going to get there.

Your 'action plan' will need to include the objectives and goals for your new business venture because, just like an Apollo rocket, your business not only needs a mission, but it must have a clear destination too. If you don't set down your goals for yourself and your business, how will you know when you have achieved them?

To help you maintain a healthy cash flow, let's now complete the 'Operational Cash Flow' template that you can use to monitor your business's financial performance.

OPERATIONAL CASH FLOW

You can use Google Sheets or Excel to easily create the following template, or most accounting software platforms, like Xero, offer ways to track your financial performance.

Begin by completing the first column (go back to the end of Chapter 5 where you completed your 'Financial Planning' and add these figures to column one), then track your income and expenses each month thereafter...

	Month 1	Month 2	Month 3
Income			
Investment			
Sales			
Total (in)			

Expenses			
Materials			
Contractors			
Marketing			
Legal			
Accounting			
Equipment			
Wages			
Other costs			
Total (out)			

Net Cash Flow			
Tax provision			
Balance			

DAY

14

GETTING THE BALANCE RIGHT

We have just one more day to go before you jump into the pilot's seat and flick the ignition switch for your new business venture. There is just one more chapter to cover, and that chapter is all about getting the balance right.

Running a business can be one of the most demanding and stressful times of your life if you don't manage it correctly. You probably already have quite a demanding life. You may have children with sporting commitments, school fees to pay, a mortgage, jobs and chores around the home, family events, the need to keep up with technology, insurance to pay, car maintenance, and so on. On top of all of this, you are now about to add the ongoing demands that a business will bring to your life: customers, taxes, financial management, staff or suppliers, increased communications (phone, email, web), sales and marketing, and, after all this, actually doing the work for which you want to get paid!

It may sound like a lot – and, of course, it is – but it's all achievable as long you get the balance right. Almost a fifth of Australians are now self-employed, so it certainly can be done.[1]

BALANCING THE WHEEL OF LIFE

Learning how to juggle your work and family comfortably is no easy task, especially when your focus is on setting up your own business. If you take measures and are creative about the integration of your work commitments and family life, you can become a successful business leader without sacrificing your personal obligations.

To determine how your work-life balance is right now, you need to take a 'helicopter view' of your life so you can see what areas may be out of balance. This is where the Wheel of Life (or Life Wheel) can help. The Lamas of Tibet say that it was the Buddha himself who originated the Wheel of Life, forming it on the Earth with grains of rice from a rice field schoolroom. This ancient tool, commonly used by professional life coaches, helps you consider and assess each area of your life, in turn, to identify areas that need more attention.

Back in Chapter 7 you completed the blank circle that was divided into eight equal segments that, together, represent the state of balance in your life right now. The segments are labelled as follows:

- Health
- Family
- Finance
- Recreation

- Career
- Personal Development
- Friends
- Spiritual

The centre of the circle scores a one, and the outside or circumference rates a ten.

With all the points together, what did you see? If this is your 'wheel', how bumpy is the ride? Which areas of your life need the most attention? By smoothing out the wheel and improving on the lower scoring areas of your life, you will effectively achieve better balance and stability.

A HEALTHY BODY, A HEALTHY MIND

One thing is for sure – you are going to need boundless energy to create your business and manage it day to day. A healthy body and a healthy mind will ensure that you ultimately build a healthy business. You have to remember that you are not merely an employee anymore. There will be no more sick leave when you don't feel well, and there will not be someone to do your job for you when you can't make it in. If you don't work, the business doesn't operate, and you don't get paid.

Today's modern health you when you are sick, they practitioners believe in the haven't been doing their job philosophy that if they see properly. The new strategy is for preventative health management. Your complete family history, your current level of fitness, and your lifestyle influences are assessed and an 'executive health plan' is designed. Before you embark on the exciting journey ahead, take the time to visit your doctor for a complete 'health check' and put in place a plan to help you stay in optimum health at all times.

Make a commitment to yourself to focus on your health, and the results will shine through in your business. A few areas to consider for your health plan:

- **Flu prevention** – The average Australian worker takes ten days of sick leave per year, costing the economy billions of dollars.[2] 'Taking a sickie' is no longer an option when you have your own business, so consider getting the flu vaccination every year to help prevent, or at least reduce, flu symptoms.

- **Healthy diet** – You have heard the saying, "You are what you eat," so make sure you eat well and limit the intake of processed and fast foods. When you are busy working or under stress, it is easy to fall into the trap of eating quick, easy meals. You should maintain a healthy weight, and a well-balanced diet can help you do this. Books like *The Good Enough Diet*, by health industry dietitian Tara Diversi and exercise physiologist Dr Adam Fraser, can help produce great results for people who want to be healthy but don't have time to be obsessive. This book is packed with a series of easy-to-implement strategies to deliver weight loss results without turning your lifestyle upside down!

- **Personal training** – If you aren't already a member of your local gym, then it's time to join! Kickstart your fitness regime with a few personal training sessions, a few active classes, or aim to walk 10,000 steps a day. Having others around you, like a personal trainer, will motivate you and ensure you get the most out of every session. Virtually any form of exercise – from aerobics to weightlifting – can help you relieve stress and make you more productive during the working day. Regular exercise contributes to production of the brain's feel-good neurotransmitters known as 'endorphins', sheds the tensions of the day, clears the mind, and increases self-confidence. You will also notice that your quality of sleep, which can be disrupted by stress, depression, and anxiety, improves and you feel a sense of being in command of your body and life.

- **Meditate and rejuvenate** – Relaxation techniques can substantially reduce the effects of stress on the mind and body. Spending a few minutes per day in quiet meditation can slow your heart rate, lower your blood pressure, reduce muscle tension, and improve concentration. Attend a weekly meditation class, purchase a soft music album that comes with meditating exercises, or search the net for a variety of relaxation techniques.

STRIVE FOR HAPPINESS

"Happiness is a conscious choice,
not an automatic response."
- *Mildred Barthel*

If this statement is true, why would you ever choose to be sad or depressed when you can make a conscious decision to be happy?

Although events and people can influence our decision to be happy or not, it is up to us to choose how we react and how long we stay in that chosen state. We need to strive for happiness in our lives, including in our working lives. When bad things happen, we need to learn how to take steps to focus on the positive and not let temporary setbacks get us down.

Harvard reported that a study in *Proceedings of the National Academy of Sciences* found that people who had higher levels of optimism had a longer life span and a greater chance of living past age 85. The researchers analysed data from about 70,000 women and 1,400 men. For both men and women, higher levels of optimism were associated with a longer life span and "exceptional longevity."[3]

Whatever the relationship, be it at work or pleasure, people generally like to be around happy people and have a tendency to avoid those who aren't happy.

DON'T FORGET TO SMELL THE ROSES

Half of the reward of building a successful business is in the journey of getting there. If you are always just focused on the finish line, you will eventually get there, but success can be a lonely prize if you've lost your family and friends on the way. At the end of each year, or when you achieve a goal or milestone in your business growth, take the time to celebrate, reward yourself, and thank the people who are important to you – the people who helped you get where you are.

To effectively run your business and create the perfect work-life balance, you will need a diary. Whether you choose a traditional desk diary, a personal organiser, or one of the many software solutions, such as the native calendar apps on your smartphone or computer, your diary will become your trusted personal assistant. Keep a record in your calendar of family events, fitness sessions, and times to work on your business as though they are appointments and give them all the same degree of importance as you would a big meeting with a client. When you plan the week ahead, remember your 'Wheel of Life' and make sure the spokes of your wheel are even to ensure a smooth ride in all areas of your life.

RELAX ABOUT TAX

You can eliminate a lot of bumps, pitfalls, and obstacles from your road to success if you keep your eye on the dashboard. Your business is like a car on a journey: the 'odometer' shows the kilometres travelled or, in business terms, the lessons you have learned and your accomplishments. Your 'fuel gauge' indicates your energy levels – you won't go far on an empty tank! Listening to the engine and knowing when to change gear, accelerate, or slow down, deciding when it is time to change direction or even when to pick up a few passengers to help share the load – it's all very similar to running a business. Every so many thousands of kilometres, or every few months, you book your car in for a service. In the same way, your business should have a financial check-up with an accountant at least once per year. You should review the financial performance of the business every month, the same as you would check the oil and water in your car.

Understand the basics of bookkeeping so you can

read the numbers. Put simply, a business's bookkeeping system tracks the money coming in against the money going out. The basic math tells you that you won't be able to keep your doors open for long if more is going out the door than is coming in. If you are not a 'numbers' person, then do a short TAFE course on business financial management and hire a bookkeeper to manage your money. It will be the best long-term investment you could make in your business.

Finally, as the saying goes, "Two things in life are certain: death and taxes." One way or another, you will end up paying taxes, either when they are due or later, with penalties and interest fees added. The more you earn and the more successful your business is, the more tax you will need to pay. Having a relationship with a switched-on accountant will help reduce your tax threshold by spreading your income across a family trust or offsetting expenses against it. In Australia, there are other taxes that may also apply to your business, including goods and services tax (GST), payroll tax, and capital gains tax.

DON'T FORGET TO ADD SOME 'ME' TIME

Starting a business can be like unleashing a wild beast: once you let it loose, it can become extremely hard to control. Never lose sight of the underlying reasons why you started your business, whether it be to have the freedom to be your own boss, to create greater wealth, or simply to make a difference in the community. Whatever the reason, you must remain in control. You own the business; it doesn't own you.

I have been self-employed now for over 30 years, starting, selling, and even closing countless businesses during this time. I have been the chairman of a local business chamber and national president for a national not-for-profit (NFP), while running a business. I have successfully secured a $500,000 investment for one startup business and merged another to create a global business of over 80 people with offices in Australia, North America, and Ireland. I am developing a number of television projects and conducting weekly radio interviews across Australia, and I have also written this book. Above all this, I have a wonderful wife, two amazing children (and a dog called Nelson) with whom I love spending time. Yet I still find some 'me' time in among all this. Recently, I completed a six-month 'presenting to camera' course at NIDA, the training ground of the likes of Mel Gibson, Cate Blanchett, and Baz Luhrmann.

Do something for your mind, body, and spirit and schedule yourself some 'me' time, no matter how demanding your life becomes. You can use this time to work on your passions, your interests, and your dreams. Try scheduling a weekly 'hour of power' if you're struggling to make time for yourself. A few years ago, I worked with an executive coach to create a 12-month plan to achieve three specific goals – writing this book was one of those goals. I started with a 'power hour' at the start and end of the day once per week, the idea being to begin a task associated with one of my goals in the morning and to complete that task in the evening. This soon grew to be one full day per week. Fridays are now my 'me' days, when I work only on achieving those specific goals.

YOUR JOURNEY BEGINS

By starting your own business, you are not only building your own self-confidence; you are about to inspire others. Without people like you, Australia's economy would be reduced by up to 80 percent. Without small business, the majority of Australians would be unemployed.

As you begin this exciting journey, never stop learning. You need to continue to grow and mature as a person as well as a business entrepreneur. When Apple's 1997 Think Different campaign was launched not long after Steve Jobs returned to the company he founded, it began with these words:

"Here's to the crazy ones, the misfits, the rebels, the troublemakers, the round pegs in the square holes... the ones who see things differently – they're not fond of rules, and they have no respect for the status quo. You can quote them, disagree with them, glorify or vilify them, but the only thing you can't do is ignore them because they change things. They push the human race forward. While some may see them as the crazy ones, we see genius, because the people who are crazy enough to think that they can change the world, are the ones who do."

Make good use of the workbook sections you have been completing throughout this book – it's now time to bring it all to life and make it happen.

You can access additional resources, advice, and support by visiting www.tonyeades.com. You can also access the 'Business Accelerator' program to take your business to the next level.

Congratulations on starting your business in 14 days! Your entrepreneurial journey begins now.

"You guys are the magicians of the 21st century. Don't let anything hold you back. Imagination is the limit. Go out there and create some magic."

ELON MUSK

WHAT'S NEXT?

We live in a world of changing technology that's impacting our lives and businesses every day. Your new business will need to be agile enough to move and flow with the changes the world brings. Artificial intelligence, robots, and automation are all becoming our new way of life.

We've all heard of the marketing funnel – and most businesses still use this as their model to attract new customers. The problem is it doesn't retain customers, so it's flawed and outdated.

We need to remove our 'funnel vision'. It's similar to tunnel vision, where we limit our potential in the new world that demands adaptability and agility.

The problem is that the funnel had been the cornerstone of a marketing strategy for over a century and was invented by E St Elmo Lewis back in the 1800s and widely regarded as the first formal theory of marketing.

Well, here's some breaking news, sorry Elmo:

"The funnel is dead... RIP."

Today, as marketers, we still need to attract leads, generate interest, and encourage engagement, to prompt decisions and action... but not necessarily in that order, and not using outdated tactics.

Would you agree that the way we buy has somewhat changed since the 1800s? Of course it has!

Back then, a typical high street directory had a confectioner, grocer, tobacconist, pub, dairyman, tripe seller, and cheesemonger all in one street. But that was it. They were your choices.

Shop assistants would serve each customer individually, and many ingredients, like butter and flour, had to be weighed and bagged by the shop staff before you could take it home.

Today, we have self-service, online ordering, home delivery, cashless payments, chatbots, and digital assistants. Yet we still use a marketing funnel from 1898.

It was time we created a new model. Something more relevant to the world of today and one that better serves your new business.

Since the 1500s, an early device for measuring intervals of time has been known as a sandglass or an hourglass.

You might even have one at home – the small ones are good for timing eggs – but, in essence, it's a simple device where sand or liquid is placed in the uppermost section and runs through the neck into the lower section in exactly one hour.

Once the journey is complete, the device is turned upside down, and the process can be continued indefinitely.

My team and I got inspired by the hourglass – we knew it was time to replace the tired, old marketing funnel and instead design a model that was more efficient and continuous in nature.

And the results have been extraordinary!

We've now created a completely new model that allows for greater flow from marketing to sales, and it orchestrates a more complete buyer journey. And it doesn't end once someone becomes a customer like the original marketing funnel did. Instead, we've created a 'delight pathway' with special offers, education, notifications, and incentives to keep customers engaged and coming back.

So, to replace the old sales and marketing funnel, we took the hourglass and decided to turn it on its head – well, on its side! What's remarkable is that once you turn the hourglass on its side, you see an infinity symbol.

Derived from the Latin word, 'infinitas', meaning endless or eternity, it's used to explain events or feelings that are eternal, boundless, and limitless.

Introducing The Infinity Track®…

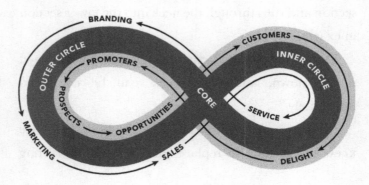

This new model enhances the methodology of inbound marketing, as coined by HubSpot co-founder, Brian Halligan.

There are two parts to your Infinity Track®. On the left is the outer circle. This is everything that is outside of your business – your marketing, your brand, your positioning.

The inner circle on the right is everything inside your business – your people, your culture, your services, and your technology

Now, both circles have to work in harmony with each other to succeed. But the real power of the Infinity Track® is right there in the centre – at its core. This is the area where both circles – inner and outer – meet in the middle and cross over. This is where your CRM sits and dashboards come to life.

Your buyer journey can seamlessly flow around both circles, with a prospect becoming an opportunity within the marketing process and ultimately the customer becoming a promoter through the sales process.

I look forward to our next book together as we build out this model for infinite growth on your business journey.

"Your time is limited, so don't waste it living someone else's life."

STEVE JOBS

ACKNOWLEDGEMENTS

I would like to acknowledge the amazing team at Dean Publishing for bringing this book to life – writing it is one thing; publishing is an entirely different experience.

My thanks to my accountant, John Richards, from Richards Financial Services for reviewing the 'boring stuff'.

Special shout-out to the talented team at Salted Stone for their support and for keeping me focused.

Thank you also to the awesome Troy and Zara, who worked with me on the development of my keynote and bringing to life The Infinity Track®.

Finally, to my family and friends who have constantly pushed me to share my story – this is for you.

ABOUT TONY

Tony is a business rethinker and brand futurist, using the combination of strategy and new technology to help businesses optimise their brand positioning, customer experience, and digital transformation. From startups to global enterprises, he is passionate about futureproofing brands and helping them engage with the new consumer and thrive in the ever-changing marketplace.

He writes for a number of publications, including *Sydney Morning Herald*, has been featured on television and radio, including Channel Nine, Triple M Network, and 2GB and also as a brand experience expert for Kochie's Business Builders – a national business TV show, which airs to an audience of 3 million, and a weekly blog, which is sent to over 100,000 small businesses across Australia.

As an international keynote speaker, he is a certified

speaking professional and speaks regularly at events across Australia, Asia, and the US. He was a past national president of Professional Speakers Australia and is currently the chief strategy officer at Salted Stone, a global award-winning digital marketing agency and HubSpot Elite Partner of over 80 people, with offices in APAC, NA, and EMEA.

To connect with Tony, go to **tonyeades.com**

or via LinkedIn, go to **https://www.linkedin.com/in/tonyeades**

ENDNOTES

DAY 1

1 Inside Small Business 2022, *Almost Half of New Businesses Failing within Their First Four Years*, online article, Octomedia, Sydney, viewed 12 February 2023, https://insidesmallbusiness.com.au/latest-news/almost-half-of-new-businesses-fail-within-their-first-four-years.

2 Australian Small Business and Family Enterprise Ombudsman 2022, *Contribution to Australian Business Numbers*, online report, ASBFEO, Canberra, viewed 13 February 2023, https://www.asbfeo.gov.au/contribution-australian-business-numbers.

DAY 2

1 Gerber, ME 2009, *The E-Myth: Why Most Businesses Don't Work and What to Do About It*, HarperCollins, Sydney.

2 Mangalindan, JP 2012, *Amazon's Recommendation Secret*, online article, Fortune, New York City, viewed 13 February 2023, https://fortune.com/2012/07/30/

amazons-recommendation-secret/.

DAY 6

1 Horovitz, B & Tassy, E 1993, *Jury Award Ends Domino's 30-Minute Delivery Pledge*, online article, Los Angeles Times, El Segundo, viewed 19 February 2023, https://www.latimes.com/archives/la-xpm-1993-12-22-mn-4588-story.html.

DAY 7

1 Solomon, M 2016, *Consumer Behaviour: Buying, Having, and Being*, 12 edn, Pearson, London.

2 Todorov, A 2017, *Face Value: The Irresistible Influence of First Impressions*, Princeton University Press.

3 Farber, B 2007, *Listen and Learn When Making a Sale*, online article, Entrepreneur, Irvine, viewed 19 February 2023, https://www.entrepreneur.com/growing-a-business/listen-and-learn-when-making-a-sale/173380.

4 National Commission on Writing for America's Families, Schools, and Colleges 2004, *Writing: A Ticket to Work… Or a Ticket Out*, online report, College Board, New York, viewed 19 February 2023, http://www.u.arizona.edu/~mwalker/CommisionReportSummary.pdf.

5 Hill, N 1938, *Think and Grow Rich*, The Ralston Society, Meriden, Connecticut, p 35.

6 Ibid.

7 Image on page 115 – Concept was originally created by Paul J. Meyer, founder of Success Motivation® Institute, Inc.

DAY 9

1 Mission Statement Academy n.d., *Domino's Mission and Vision Statement Analysis*, online article, UCLA, Los Angeles, viewed 20 February 2023, https://mission-statement.com/dominos/.

DAY 11

1 Bank of Queensland 2023, *The Top 10 Reasons Small Businesses Fail – and How to Avoid Them*, online article, BOQ, Brisbane, https://www.boq.com.au/business/small-business/business-knowledge-hub/opening-a-small-business/the-top-ten-reasons-small-businesses-fail.

2 Ibid.

3 Norquay, J 2023, *Australian Internet Statistics 2023*, online article, Prosperity Media, Surry Hills, viewed 22 February 2023, https://prosperitymedia.com.au/australian-internet-statistics/. Durkin, P 2022, *Australians Spent a Record $62b Online – and It's Set to Double*, online article, Australian Financial Review, Sydney, viewed 22 February 2023, https://www.afr.com/companies/retail/australians-spent-a-record-62b-online-and-it-s-set-to-double-20220404-p5aaoi.

4 Digital.com 2022, *1 in 2 Visitors Abandon a Website That Takes More Than 6 Seconds to Load*, online report, viewed 22 February 2023, https://blog.kissmetrics.com/wp-content/uploads/2011/04/loading-time.pdf.

5 Hudgens, R, 2023, *152 Must-know Marketing Statistics*, webpage, Siege Media, San Diego, viewed 18 October 2023, https://www.siegemedia.com/strategy/content-marketing-statistics.

DAY 12

1   Day, M 2020, *Marketing in a Recession: The Best
    Performing Tech Companies of the Next Five Years Have
    Already Increased Their Marketing Budgets*, online article,
    Marketing Moves, Shepperton, viewed 19 February
    2023, https://www.marketingmoves.com/2020/05/
    marketing-in-a-recession-best-performing-tech-
    companies-of-the-next-five-years-have-already-
    increased-their-marketing-budgets/.

2   Lipovich, I 2021, *Building Brand Recognition Through Your
    Content and BI Tools*, online article, Forbes, Jersey City,
    viewed 24 February 2023, https://www.forbes.com/
    sites/forbesbusinesscouncil/2021/08/20/building-
    brand-recognition-through-your-content-and-bi-
    tools/?sh=2344972d3894.

3   Macrotrends 2023, *CocaCola Net Worth 2010-2022 | KO*,
    online report, viewed 24 February 2023, https://www.
    macrotrends.net/stocks/charts/KO/cocacola/net-
    worth.

4   Clark, J 2020, *The AFL's Marketing from the 1970s
    to Today*, online article, Jackson Clark Media,
    Darwin, viewed 19 February 2023, https://www.
    jacksonclarkmedia.com.au/post/the-afl-s-marketing-
    from-the-1970s-to-today.

5   Tourism and Events Queensland n.d., *Best Job in the
    World*, webpage, Fortitude Valley, viewed 24 February
    2023, https://teq.queensland.com/au/en/industry/
    what-we-do/marketing/best-job-in-the-world.

6   Internet Live Stats 2023, *In One Second, Each and Every
    Second, There Are…*, interactive webpage, viewed 19

February 2023, https://www.internetlivestats.com/
one-second/#google-band.

7 Ibid.

8 Hughes, C 2022, *Average Time Spent Online by Internet
Users in Australia December 2019 by age group*, online
article, Statista, Hamburg, viewed 12 February 2023,
https://www.statista.com/statistics/1111450/australia-
average-total-time-spent-online-by-active-internet-
users-by-age-group/#:~:text=In%20December%20
2019%2C%20active%20internet%20users%20ag-
ed%20between,18%20to%2024%20spent%20
around%2088.5%20hours%20online.

DAY 13

1 Inside Small Business 2022, *Almost Half of New
Businesses Failing within Their First Four Years*, online
article, Octomedia, Sydney, viewed 25 February 2023,
https://insidesmallbusiness.com.au/latest-news/
almost-half-of-new-businesses-fail-within-their-first-
four-years.

DAY 14

1 Self-Employed Australia 2022, *Independent
Contractors: How Many in Australia?*, online report,
Melbourne, viewed 25 February 2023, https://
selfemployedaustralia.com.au/independent-
contractors-how-many/independent-contractors-how-
many-in-australia/.

2 Jolly, W 2019, *Australian Economy Could Lose $7 Billion
to Sick Days in 2019*, online article, Savings.com.au,
Brisbane, viewed 25 February 2023, https://www.

savings.com.au/news/australian-economy-could-lose-7-billion-to-sick-days-in-2019.

3 Lee, LO, James, P, Zevon, ES, Kim, ES, Trudel-Fitzgerald, C, Spiro, A, 3rd, Grodstein, F & Kubzansky, LD 2019, 'Optimism is associated with exceptional longevity in 2 epidemiologic cohorts of men and women', *Proceedings of the National Academy of Sciences of the United States of America*, vol 116, no 37, pp 18357-18362, viewed 9 February 2023, https://doi.org/10.1073/pnas.1900712116.

If you loved this book, then connect with us at Dean Publishing for more great reads or publishing tips.

DEAN
PUBLISHING

deanpublishing.com